FROM EVERTON VALE TO RIVINGTON PIKE

MY SLICE OF LIFE

*To Shiela
with much love
Edith
17.6.09*

An autobiography by
Edith Amy Pierce

© Edith Amy Pierce 2008
All rights reserved.

ISBN 978-1-4092-5166-8

Foreword

The following stories are true. I have written them as I remember them, although not everybody remembers each event in the same way. If you have played a part in any of these stories, please do not be offended if my version is not quite how you recall it!

I have changed some names, where I have not been able to contact the people involved for their permission.

You can find out more, and listen to some of my stories online at

www.mysliceoflife.synthasite.com

If you have any additions or comments, please feel free to contact me at

mysliceoflife@gmx.com

Edith Amy Pierce
June 2008

Contents

Foreword 5
Contents 6
Prologue 9
The Jerseys 12
High Days and Holidays 19
Christmas Stuffing 21
Rawcliffe Road 23
Bikes 24
Packs of trouble 28
A Fine Romance 31
Childhood Visits 35
The Joys of Life! 37
The Tunnel 39
The Start of War 41
Is Guinness Good for You? 42
Next Best Thing to an Organist 46
Early War Time 50
Sweater and Helmet 52
Gone with the Wind 54
Exmouth 55
Hero's Return 58
Arthur Gosby Pierce 60
A New Family 61
War from Post War Perspective 63
Post War Britain 65
Mad Dog and Ankle 67
Kenneth 68
The Middle One 70
Roof Repairs 71
A Right Royal 'Do' 73
The Isle of Man 75
Family of Three 78
Operations 80
The Great Fire 83
Dentist 87
Hong Kong 88
Buckingham Palace 90

Mum and Dad	91
Brenda, Marjorie and President Kennedy	92
On the Edge	93
A Testing Time	95
Scotland for the Brave	98
Stopping the Traffic	105
Cornwall - Launceston	107
Marjorie	110
Joyce	113
Jeannette	115
Arnside	118
The Family Scattering	120
The Next Generation	121
The End of an Era	128
The C.H.A	135
A New Start	138
Marjorie's New Start	141
More About the Family	147
Sisters and Brothers	152
Life with John	156
Eventful Walks	159
Caravan Capers	166
An Accident	167
Marjorie and Philip	169
A Knitting Nancy	175
Rule of Thumb	177
The tables are turned	181
Epilogue	187

E.A.Pierce June 2008

Prologue

On one of my walks recently, I visited the Memorial Pinetum at Rivington. There are two very special trees there which I planted about eleven years ago and I like to check on their progress from time to time. They are both looking very healthy and growing strongly I am pleased to report. Whilst standing there, my mind is flooded with so many memorable events from my past life, happy, exciting, sad or tragic.

My life has not been out of the ordinary but I have lived through extraordinary times and have always enjoyed telling a good tale. Living in the 20th Century when life moved on so quickly from only bicycles or horses for transport to trains, cars, aeroplanes and space travel, has brought much change and plenty of stories to tell. I have been blessed with three daughters and they have urged me on many occasions to record my stories so that the grandchildren and great grandchildren will better understand life with all its twists and turns

Early Days

I was born Edith Amy Whiteway on March 22nd 1919, the fourth child, in the midst of a pneumonia epidemic, in Liverpool.

At the time of my birth, my father, Reginald, arrived home very ill with pneumonia. The doctor was sent for to see dad just as my mother, Edith, went into labour, so the midwife was also called. Dad had a bed downstairs and his mother came and cared for and nursed him. I believe she found it a 'nightmare', my sisters were five and three years old and my brother was only 18 months older than me and he was trying to go up and down the stairs; my grandmother had her work cut out. Of course, mothers were kept in bed for two weeks after childbirth then.

Rather sadly, my grandmother caught the pneumonia and as there were no antibiotics, she died within a month. The family had to face the crisis, dad was sent into hospital and mother had to ask her father to help as her own mother was deceased. However, dad did get better and life carried on although he wasn't fit for work for a few weeks and men did not get any sick pay wages then. Luckily, my mother had a kind brother, in a steady position, living in Hoylake on the Wirral, who helped her financially until dad was well and back to work.

So then there was Laura, the eldest, who would be about six years old, then Ida the next at four and a half years, Reg my brother at 18 months, me, and 22 months later my younger sister, Gladys arrived. We lived in a terraced house in Windermere Street in Everton Vale, Liverpool, with three bedrooms, sitting room and kitchen. We called the sitting room our 'parlour', complete with aspidistra. It was about three miles from the city which was a great shipping town then with liners sailing up and down the river Mersey, crisscrossed by ferry boats to Rock Ferry, Seacombe and New Brighton.

The Jerseys

We became a family of five children with mum and dad. We had quite a normal style of life, my dad was a fully apprenticed joiner and my mother descended from parents who dealt in a business, really a cottage industry. It was connected to the Merchant Navy as Liverpool was a great seafaring town, and began in the 19th century. It was customary for the sailors to wear navy blue knitted jerseys with polo necks, with the company logo embroidered across the front. The officers were in navy blue suits with gold bullion embroidery on caps and epaulettes. All this embroidery was done by hand and each batch had to be completed and delivered to the docks before the ship sailed. It was a real family business as all the lettering and shapes had to be cut out of cardboard and glued on to the jerseys by the men before the stitching could be completed by the girls.

This business my mother inherited. When she was growing up they employed a few girls and taught them to embroider. Mother's sister was a teacher and her brother a director; consequently, they weren't interested in sewing. So after her parents died, mum and our family carried on with it, which was a good advantage then because jobs were hard to get, especially one you would like to do. It was only a small cottage industry which started in my grandfather's time. It really flourished in the 1930's, when Liverpool was a thriving seafaring town with miles of docks.

We could go to the Pier Head, near the Liver Buildings, the Mersey Docks and Harbour Board and the Cunard Steamship Company, all huge buildings on the sea front, and get the overhead railway along the dock road to see all the huge liners loading or offloading exports and imports from round the world. It was a train mainly for the dock labourers to get to and from work. Those ships all had timetables for sailing and the freight had to be in the holds on time. Eventually, in the 1960's, all the

E.A.Pierce June 2008

big shipping went down to Southampton and the overhead railway was demolished.

On the jerseys, everything was sewn by hand with the shipping company's name on the top, crossed flags in the middle and place of destination underneath.

Display exemplar, recently embroidered by Edith

Set with a stencil, we did 1" (one inch or 2.5 cm) white embroidered letters. The flags were white with a red cross and blue with a white cross and a small gold silk crown in the centre of the white flag. My father made the stencil and cut all the letters out. He made a box with little sections which held all the letters and boiled up a big pot of fish glue to set them on with. That was apart from his own job.

When my brother was old enough, he had to do this sometimes, but he hated it. All of us girls were taught how to embroider the letters in white wool.

This business came along in batches; we would receive about 6 dozen, all in separate parcels with 6 jerseys in each and we would have to have the order completed and on the ship two hours before it sailed. My dad would hire a taxi with all 6 dozen, wrapped in brown paper and tied up with string, and take them to the dock to be loaded, then the bill would be taken to the Liver Buildings and we would be paid.

We were the only people in Liverpool who carried this business forward. I have seen the time when we have had a telegram to come home from holiday, when we were teenagers, to get an order through. We couldn't grumble because we all received new clothes and any extras we needed and it was a great help towards expenses.

Schooldays

We all in turn went to Granton Road School, the state school that was the nearest. It was a very strict school and children had to be seen and not heard. Going into classes, we all lined up in the playground and marched into classrooms.

One day, a little boy in the infants was sick whilst walking in and the teacher shouted at him and nearly made him clean it up himself. The next day he was in hospital with diphtheria.

When I was in the third year infants, we were learning how to fold coloured paper and make shapes. In the middle of the lesson, the teacher went out of the classroom and of course all the children started talking, but as soon as she came back, it was dead silence. She said,

> "Anyone who talked while I was out of the room, put your hand up."

Well, being taught honesty at home, I put my hand up, the only one!
I was sent to the headmistress, as punishment she made me stand by her desk with my hands on my head for ages. She wouldn't even let me go to the toilet at playtime. So, when I went home at dinner time (as all children did then) and told my mother, she went up to the school and told the headmistress it was a prison warden she should be, not an infant head.

She then decided that all of us five children would change schools to the church school, Holy Trinity, as it was 'more civilised'. So, the following Monday, she took all five of us to Holy Trinity school and had us sorted into different classes. Later, it was said she looked just like a hen with all her chicks under her wings.

To me, it seemed just like a church and I was frightened that I would not be picked up at 4 o'clock. It turned out to be a school with much more understanding and a kinder atmosphere, but I must also add that it wasn't as advanced in reading, writing and sums. I had already reached a higher grade than the class I was put in.

This school had a lovely swing park at the back and a library close by and we did all our games lessons in the park grounds. We also joined the church Sunday School and were given little text cards to take home each week. The school went into church once a week during Lent and I can still see the vicar, Mr. Barrow, standing in the pulpit at harvest time, (so it was all decorated with grapes) saying to us,

"Keep looking at me in case I eat all these grapes."

The Sunday School organised outings. We went by train from Clubmore Station over the Runcorn Bridge to Helsby Hills. We were given a bag with sandwiches and cake for our lunch and we played games and races. It always seemed to be a sunny day. This church also had Guides and Brownies and Boy's Brigade. My eldest sister Laura, known as Lol, decided she was joining the Guides, so of course when we grew old enough, we joined Brownies and then Guides.

We had an incident in our class when I was about 8 years old. We were sewing fancy samples or knitting when one of the girls at the front said she had lent her pen, which had been a special gift to her, to the girl sitting next to her, and now could not find it. Well, the search for this pen went on until we were all involved, so everyone had to be searched. We all had to stand on our seats and take our shoes off.

Well, that morning, I couldn't find my socks, so I pinched my brother's, but they were a lot bigger so I had the toes folded underneath. I was mortified at having to take my shoes off as teacher came to each one and searched them, in the shoes as well. However, when the pen had not been found, the search went into all the wool and material. The teacher picked up the girl's ball of wool and could feel an object and discovered it was the pen. She was in dire trouble! None of us was allowed to speak to that girl for a week; we called it 'sent to Coventry'. I wonder does she ever look back on that day.

I had another friend, who lived in the house opposite to us, her name was Annie. She had just one brother. She had started music lessons, so I asked my mum if I could start as well. It was a long way up Breck Road, near the top. It didn't cost so much, so I went with her for three years and could then play the piano fairly well.

School was not too bad for me. I was always told I could do better, but I was far more fond of fun and outdoor activities than to sit at home to do homework and study. Ida was the most academic in our family. She passed the exams and followed a nursing career, ending up as Principal Midwifery Tutor.

During school days, time was coming round to sit for the scholarship. Not many children did pass scholarships in those days, mainly the rich, and if the poorer child was clever enough to pass for the grammar school, they were given free books and dinners. So they were looked down upon by the rich, when they were probably cleverer, having gained the place through a lot more effort. However, we had to sit the review first and if we passed that, we then had to go to sit the scholarship at the grammar school. I may add that I did pass the review, but not the scholarship as I was not very bothered. My friend passed and went to the grammar school but I carried on at my school until I was 14 years old.

Family Life

We were a family unit. We didn't have anything to spare, but enough to go round. We all had a turn of having our shoes mended. My dad being handy at most jobs that needed mending in the house, would come home every Saturday with a length of shoe leather and ask whose shoes needed repairing. He would then put this leather in to soak in cold water to make it pliable. After his dinner, he would get his last out and whosoever turn it was would have to sit on the sofa until their shoes were done before going out.

My father, Reginald Whiteway

Friday night was bath night and we had a large tin bath that hung on the backyard wall. It had to be filled with water boiled on the gas ring in the kitchen. Then one at a time we had turns, while the rest of the family sat in the parlour and we had a good scrubbing each.

Our main washing was always done on a Monday with scrubbing board and blue dolly dye for the white clothes. It was nearly a full day's work. When we came home at dinner time from school, there was always washing everywhere and we always had leftovers from Sunday's roast for dinner; I hated it!

My father loved birds and being a joiner, he made bird boxes which fitted into each side of the fireplace. They went up to the ceiling and were filled with canaries, they were lovely.

When we had birthdays, we only ever had one present off our parents, not like today when all family and friends give presents. Well, my birthday came near Easter, so I had an auntie, (who used to come and teach us to play the piano), who always gave me a chocolate Easter egg; that was very special.

When I was about twelve years old, my mother became very ill. It started with gall stones but she had complications, so she was taken to hospital and was in for weeks. Now my sister Ida (next to eldest) was always quite motherly and kindly, she gave up her job to look after us. She would be only about sixteen and a half years old but she cooked, washed and shopped whilst going in to visit mum most days. It was very serious at one point. However, she did recover and Ida could go back to work.

We all had different jobs to do at home then. Gladys and I had to use emery paper, sitting each side of the fire to rub all the rusty marks off the fender. If water dripped on, it went a bit rusty. Reg had to do the cutlery as they too weren't silver. Ida did some washing up.
Laura had to scrub the wooden seat of the toilet at the bottom of the yard. Talking about the toilet, ours was a pain to go to, after it had gone dark. It was at the very bottom of the yard, so we asked if someone would come with us, and take a little candle. During the night, it had to be a bucket on the landing, but that was the usual practice then.

We weren't a quiet family; we played games and sometimes one cheated, so we would argue and fight, then my dad would come in and we would run upstairs and scramble under a double bed. He, being very agile, could run up two stairs at a time and with a stick he would be rapping the bed side, pretending to reach us underneath. We would be getting as far back as we could and pushing the weakest to the front. At other times, if he was at work, and my mother was having a rest in bed and a rumpus broke out, we would just hear my mother's footsteps (in slippers) coming down, we immediately scattered.

When we were children, my dad made us a beautiful large rocking horse with a strong, solid plinth to withstand the rocking to and fro. It was complete with stirrups and horsehair mane and tail. We all used and enjoyed it. One takes so much for granted as children. I think now of the work that went into making that horse. It went right down the family; my brother ended up with it for his children and grandchildren. It may still be in existence now!

He also made a swing with iron rings to hang onto two big hooks in the doorway between the back kitchen and the yard. We could swing quite high there. Again, it was used by the grandchildren in Rawcliffe Road.

Some of Dad's workmanship as a joiner still remains in Liverpool. He made the three storey banister rail for the Crane Theatre. It was about two feet wide in beautiful oak, all finished in a fine varnish. He also made some of the heavy double locking bank doors throughout the city. He became a staircase specialist and I remember being told of his trip to Lille, in France, before I was born, where he made the communion rail and pulpit with stairs curving up, for the cathedral there.

High Days and Holidays

As a young family growing up, we were always taken out for the day on bank holidays. We could get the ferryboat to New Brighton or Seacombe and walk along the promenades or play on the sands. We also had the choice of the ferry followed by a bus across the Wirral to Hoylake, West Kirby or Moreton, all with seaside fronts. So, mum would prepare a pile of sandwiches and biscuits to take with us while dad sat Gladys and me on the kitchen draining board (with a ridge under our knees) and scrubbed our hands and knees, and then we were all ready for off.

We played in the sea whilst mum minded all the clothes and dad taught us how to swim. Then, on the beaches, were huts selling pots of tea. One had to pay about 10d for a large pot, but there was also a deposit on the teapot and cups, which we got back when we returned them. Going back home, we had to stand together at the Pier Head, which was the bus terminus. There were hundreds of families waiting to get the bus home, and no queuing in those days, so as a bus came, my dad would gather all of us in front of him and heave us all together onto the bus steps and off for home. Us young ones would run up the stairs of the bus and sit in the section at the back, the bit without the roof, then we would all arrive home, quite sunburnt.

Each year, for four years, my mother booked a week's holiday on a farm during the school holidays. The farm was on the Wirral, just outside Moreton. As well as the animals, it had an orchard in the grounds where we enjoyed lots of fun. From the farm was a long country path which led down to the sea front, very near the lighthouse. We could wander up and down, no fear of us being lost or picked up. My dad had to get to work each day from this holiday farm because workmen did not get any holiday pay and we depended on his wages.

Where we lived in Windermere Street, Liverpool, it was typical of the working class. Most of the property was rented and it was easier to change address, particularly if anyone wasn't satisfied with the house they rented because of a leaky roof or faulty windows, etc. which the landlord would not have mended. Then they would get a large handcart and pack most of their possessions, stack it high, tie it all together and walk off to another rented house. However, people did not have so many possessions then. Sometimes, if a family was being sued for non payment of rent, they just moved off and disappeared.

Our neighbourhood was okay, quite friendly. I, as a child, played out in the street most nights. I can remember my sister Laura getting a second hand bicycle, I must only have been about 7 or 8 but when she was out, I would take her bike and ride up and down the street on the pedals, as I could not reach the seat. Then, if she found out, I would be in trouble!

Growing up, I was pretty tough, not a timid child, but not cheeky. I played with Gladys quite a lot, and was always keen to play out, maybe because I was closest in age to my older brother, Reg.

Christmas Stuffing

It was Christmas morning at home. We had woken early but, as I have said before, on special occasions we only ever had presents from our parents as that was all anyone could afford. At Christmas we had our usual orange, chocolate shape and new penny in a stocking with a toy and a box of sweets, everyone was satisfied and happy enough. Often, my dad had made the toys out of wood, like a little cart with a long handle, on wheels, or a little chair. I also remember he made a dolls' pram in wood, which went down the family, it was so solid.

In the past few weeks we had all helped mum and mixed all the things that go in Christmas puddings and added two silver sixpenny pieces. We all had to stir and make a wish, then it was tied up, ready for boiling. At another time we made paper chains for decorations, cutting up coloured paper into strips.

Our usual Christmas dinner was chicken, with stuffing all made with bread, onion, sage and boiling water. Now this Christmas morning, I had been playing out and I went into the house to look for something. I can't remember now what it was, but it entailed me climbing up on the sink edge to reach the shelf above, which most kitchens had in those days.

As it was Christmas morning, my dad had mixed the stuffing for the chicken and left it in its basin to cool in the sink. He had then gone off to see to his birds that he kept. As I was reaching up to this shelf, there was a packet of soapflakes by my hand. I accidentally caught the packet and it fell, emptying soap flakes into the stuffing. I knew there would not be any extra to make more. I was terrified when I saw what I had done and ran out through the front door.

I was always a fast runner, so I ran and ran. I had no idea of the time and it must have been near dinner time when I saw Laura turning towards me, so of course I ran further away. She went back home, then about half an hour later, Laura and Reg came along shouting to me, saying,

"My dad won't smack you if you come home."

So they took me home and I was relieved, but I couldn't face much dinner!

To cook a full dinner, we used a black range with a big fireplace. We had to build up the fire and push it under the back of the oven with a large poker until it was very hot. Everything went into the oven; meat, roast potatoes, rice pudding. Then my mother would mix a big fruit cake and put that on a tray in the oven.

The money was only ever just enough to go round. Mum had accounts at the butchers, the greengrocers and Dimwoody's, a home made bakery, so we bought things 'on tick'. On Monday morning she would pay off the bills and have about 3d left for the rest of the week. I think we ate well though, and had a healthy diet.

Another funny episode was when we had run out of currants, mum sent Laura to go for a packet. Well, she loved currants and when she came back my dad opened the door and noticed that the packet was not full. He asked,

> "What's happened to the currants?"

He gave her a sharp tap on the back but she had a mouthful of them and they shot out of her mouth, up the hallway!

Rawcliffe Road

We were now growing up to our teens as a family and my mother wanted a better neighbourhood for us, so whilst my dad was at work, she went with Ida to look at some houses on what was then the outskirts of the North of Liverpool, and chose a large house in Rawcliffe Road. This was near the tram terminus at Walton, but it goes miles further up now.

We were paying 10/- (10 shillings, 50p) per week in Windermere Street and this house with 4 bedrooms, an attic and basement was 21/- (£1.05) per week. That was an upgrade, but we children had now reached working age. It had a kitchen and back kitchen, back parlour and front parlour downstairs, the bedrooms and bathroom upstairs. There were three attic bedrooms on the top floor and cellars under the kitchen. The lighting was gas, with a bracket and a mantle which was lit with a match, and all open fires in fire places in each room.

We certainly had more room and freedom. We became very friendly with the family opposite. They had two sons, Jim and Alex and one daughter, Margaret, who was called 'Peggy'. We teamed up with this family; they had bikes too. Six of us would cycle out to Southport some evenings - it was about 15 miles.

Also, Jim could play the piano, like me, and we had sing-songs around the piano.

The boys were in the Sea Scouts and we were in the Guides, so we all went to the Scout dances, parties and socials. Although we had such an enjoyable time, we didn't end up dating or settling down.

Both my parents had good singing voices; mum a soprano and dad a tenor. I may add that Gladys and Ida had very nice voices too, so I would accompany them on the piano. It was a lovely evening when friends came to visit and we all gravitated round the piano to sing a lot of the songs so popular then.

When I was about 16 years old, Ida and I joined the youth group at church, where we had lots of fun and played various games. One session it was announced that everyone had to contribute to a special social evening for entertainment. So, Ida thought she would sing 'My Hero' out of 'The Chocolate Soldier' and I would accompany her. We agreed, but believe me, it was a frightening experience! We did manage it and had the audience clapping, but between us we knew there were a few mistakes and afterwards we often laughed and said,

"Remember the night we '*murdered*' 'My Hero'!"

Bikes

On my 8th birthday I received a pair of roller skates, I was delighted and almost lived on them, skating everywhere. By this age, I had made friends with Ellen, known as Nell, who lived in the next road to me. We were in the same class in school and remained friends for life. She only had one brother. Now, she received a bicycle, second hand, for her birthday, and this was great for me. She was rather more sheltered and timid than me, so I could have rides on her bike.

One day we went to Oakfields, it was quite a hilly area, and I asked if I could ride her bike. She never hesitated in saying yes. I went down a particularly steep hill and the bike went out of control, so I turned the wheel towards the curb and crashed into the wall. Well, the front wheel buckled right in and I couldn't even wheel it back! Nell was terrified to tell her mother, so I carried the bike all the way back to her house and knocked on the door. Her mother came out and nearly hit me with the bike. However, I did say I was sorry and we did remain friends.

Talk about being in trouble!

I go back to my school days when I received a second hand bike and would ride around with my friend Ellen sitting on the seat and me on the pedals. One day we went off, on the bike all the way to Clubmore, where my Auntie and Uncle lived.

Now, this Uncle Charles would always give me a halfpenny when they visited us. The slang name for a halfpenny (which would buy 2oz of sweets) was a 'meg', and so he christened me 'Meg'. This uncle worked at the corn exchange in Liverpool in a management post and always had lots of nuts.

So I took Ellen on my bike and knocked on my aunt's door in Clubmore. My parents did not know that we had gone there but we went in and Uncle Charles gave me a big bag of nuts to take home. I was a bit scared and did not want to go home with them as I would be in trouble for going so far away. I did get told off; however, we all enjoyed the nuts!

Later on, as I now was a working girl, I wanted a new bike. I have never lost the love of the outdoors. My dad came with me to choose, Gladys came too. I decided I would pay 2/6^d (two shillings and sixpence, or half a crown, worth 12 ½ p) per week for my new bike which took me two years to pay off. I chose a Raleigh, with dropped handle bars; Gladys chose a straight bike.

I felt so proud walking home with it and I still love the smell of new rubber, which hit me going into that shop. I made full use of that bike. I learned how to mend punctures, on the road.

So one evening, I asked Gladys and Peggy if they would like to have a ride out with our new bikes to the Wirral. We took a bit of a snack with us and had made sure that we had our lamps on the bikes as the nights were drawing in earlier, and we set off. We rode to the Pier Head, then took the ferry boat over the Mersey to Birkenhead and then the bus to Moreton – it was a bit of a challenge for them. I was more advanced riding on the roads so I led most of the time, but it took longer than we thought.

Sadly I have no photographs of my new prized bike, but it looked something like this.

On arrival, we were playing around, having a paddle in the sea when we realised it was twilight. When we checked our lamps, Gladys's would not switch on, and it was illegal to ride without a headlamp. We didn't want to get in trouble with the police, but we had to ride back to the ferry terminal, so we had no choice. I decided that if I rode in front of Gladys and Peggy at the back of her, then we could manage which we did and were very lucky.

By the time the boat had set sail and we arrived back in Liverpool at the Pier Head, it was pitch dark and our problem was how to get back home. There was a train service, scarce at that time of night and we couldn't afford for all of us to pay the fare. So, we put Gladys on the train with her bike while Peggy and I cycled from the Pier Head to our area, Walton/Aintree and we arranged to meet at the local station and ride the last bit together.

E.A.Pierce June 2008

With all these arrangements, time had flown by, and it was now nearly midnight. When we turned into our road, what a surprise - the street was alive! Our parents had rung the police and all were out looking for us. You may imagine what I was called! I was grounded for a week, but all were glad to see us safe.

Another episode relating to bikes was when my mother had arranged a holiday in the heart of Wales. It was on a farm near Llangollen. All the family was going and I asked if I could have my bike sent by rail and pick it up at the local station. So that was ok and Ida had hers sent too. Peggy from over the road was joining us and her bike was sent with ours.

Well, this holiday time arrived, we got there and the farmer gave us a lift to the local station to pick up our bikes and that was fine. We rode merrily back until, driving into the farm, we had to ride through a narrow path because the slurry was on the right side. I went through first and it was a bit too narrow and rough, but I managed. Then Ida came next, but she didn't chance it, so got off and walked through. Then Peggy decided that if I could do it on the bike, so could she; but she wobbled and she fell right in the slurry!

We immediately pulled her out but she was dripping. I saw the funny side of it and started laughing. Well, the farmer's wife came out and slapped me across the face for laughing at her. We had to wash her down and I had to unpack my case and lend her fresh clothes to put on. However, we did end up having a lovely time away. I had a ride with my dad, who borrowed Ida's bike, around the Horseshoe Pass, it was glorious.

As time went on, I met another group of cyclists and we did lots of rides into Wales. We would ride to the Pier Head and go on the luggage boat across the Mersey to Rock Ferry, then cycle over Queensferry into Wales. We had panniers each side of our bikes, with sleeping bags and flasks and spent camping weekends in Rhyl and Conway.

Packs of trouble

When I joined the Guides at Holy Trinity, in order to have a uniform my mother gave me sixpence each week to pay for it, and I was very proud of that uniform. It was a super company; nothing was allowed to be done slapdash. We had patrols, with each patrol named after a flower; ours was 'Rose'. We had a patrol leader who wore a white lanyard. We had inspection with each patrol standing in a line, and sometimes the District Commissioner would inspect us when she came to present the various badges we had passed. The badges were then sewn on the left sleeve of our uniform.

I remember going to Guide camp to a place in Yorkshire in a field at the top of a hill. We went by train and the camping equipment all went by road. When all were assembled together, we had to pitch these big round tents, six to each tent. We also had a large ridge tent, a first aid tent and a cooking area.

We were all put into patrols for various duties, which changed each day, such as fire patrol, when we went out collecting fire wood to keep the campfire burning; the cook patrol where you helped to prepare the meals; latrine duty, a special section screened off for toilets; or cleaning duty, where we had to scrub the dixies clean after being used for cooking.

Captain organised most things and Lieutenant took us out for walks or arranged games. We had a trained nurse for first aid. We also had the Union Jack which was unfurled during the day. When the tents were pitched, we were all given sleeping bags and we walked to the local farm to fill our bags and pillow cases with straw and put them on the ground sheet for night time. I always loved evening. We got ready for bed, Captain said prayers called 'vespers' and we sang 'taps':-

> Day is done, gone the sun
> From the sea, from the hill,
> From the sky. All is well,
> Safely rest. God is nigh.

Then the flag would be furled and flaps of tents all closed. It was a wonderful experience. Going home, we all helped to strike the tents and pack up.

My brother joined the Boys' Brigade; Ida was now a Ranger (senior Guide). When we moved to Rawcliffe Road, it was only a short bus ride to Fazakerley, and Ida was asked to take on a Brownie pack there. It was a small church, St. Paul's, in Fazakerley where she became a Brown Owl for some years, with a Tawny Owl and pack leader. Then her Tawny Owl was moving away, so when Ida asked me if I would take her place and be a Tawny Owl, I agreed.

We did lots of work with them, outings and even a pack holiday. There was a holiday place called the 'Brownie Hut', in Moreton. It's amazing how confident one is at sixteen and nineteen! We were trained in Guiding, but not in handling the different personalities of children. We learnt a lot about children during that week. They all slept in small beds in a line, each side of the long room. We had a big kitchen to make the meals, and whilst we were in the kitchen, the things they got up to!

After dinner one afternoon, we took them for an outing by bus to Hoylake. In Hoylake they had walkways made of steel because of the sinking sands. We walked the Brownies in pairs along this walkway but there was a wide space between the hand rail and the platform.

We had one Brownie who was a little bit 'backward' (as we said then) and as we were walking through she pushed her partner, who fell through the gap into the sinking sands. Without hesitation, Ida and I went flat on our tummies, grabbed her arms and pulled her out. If we hadn't acted fast then she would have gone under as it had already reached her chest. She was so shocked, and so were we, that we had to go back and find a pool to swill all the mud off her and calm her down. I must add that we had to report that to her parents.

Another time we took them swimming to the local swimming baths. Today, one would need a trained life saver when taking Brownies swimming. Again, one Brownie pushed a younger one, who could not swim, down the chute. I could only swim a couple of lengths, but we managed to save her.

Then one of them wet the bed, so we had problems there, but it was all experience and everyone went home fit and well!

We put on a couple of displays when all the parents turned up; took them to church parade once a month, marching behind the Boys' Brigade; did lots of badge work and trainings. I think Guiding gives children a good foundation in life.

A new church had been built, called St. George's; it was in an area beyond Fazakerley where new property had been built, known as Sparrow Hall. It was like an overspill from Liverpool city centre. Both St. George's and St. Paul's were connected to the main church called St. Emmanuel's. The vicar in my time was Mr. Simmons; he was quite a popular man, middle aged, with a family.

This new church wanted to have the uniformed organisations there as it was in the middle of a new estate with lots of children. One evening whilst Ida and I were with the Brownies at St. Paul's, the curate in charge of St. George's walked in. He came to ask me if I would set up a new Brownie pack. Well, I was a bit taken aback as I was only seventeen and didn't think I was capable of doing that.

However, it went before the commissioners and the District Commissioner came to help me get it off the ground. She took me to the Guide shop where we bought all the necessary things to get started. She came each week for six weeks and I attended some organised training for Guiders each month, so we managed quite well.

Our pack meeting took place in the main room of this church. The seating was taken out and stacked for the organisations to use the room. There was a balcony all round with rooms leading off for small sessions and an organ up there. Sometimes it would be playing loudly and annoy me when I was trying to organise the Brownies.

We also had a piano which I used for songs and marches with the Brownies. The minister's name was Mr. Barrow; yes, the same as we had when I was very young at Holy Trinity, but this was his son and we vaguely remembered each other although he had been at college then. I did alright and the pack progressed. I would take them out into the woods on holidays and we would play hide and seek between the trees.

Imagine doing that in this day and age!

A Fine Romance

Now Ida had a close friend from Emmanuel Church, whose name was Mrs. Hunter. She was very devoted, what we called 'a pillar of the church' so we had to conform. I mentioned that because as the Brown Owl at St. George's, I was expected to attend the Annual General Meeting but I have always hated AGM's!

On that evening, Ida asked me if I would take a message to Mrs. Hunter as she lived in Fazakerley and it was on the way to St. George's. I cycled down, dressed in ordinary clothes for a bike ride. I called at Mrs. Hunter's and she invited me in so I thought I would not need to go on to the AGM as half an hour then passed by. I mentioned that I really should be at our AGM. She immediately looked at me and said,

"Well, you can't stay in my house if you should be at the AGM. It is your duty to be there!"

So I did what I was told, got on my bike and carried on to the meeting. I had to put my bike in the corner of the hall. The meeting was well underway, so I crept in and sat down quietly.

There was Mr. Barrow the vicar, and next to him was the organist (whom I had never seen before) taking the minutes. Sometimes when I was teaching the Brownies, I could hear the organ and choir up above and wished they would be quiet, but never saw the folks. When the various items were being discussed, this chap, taking the minutes, sounded very self important and self assured.

However, when the meeting was ended, this chap came up to me and said,

"Can I have a word with you?"

I wondered what on earth he wanted, so I put my coat on, got my bike and waited, feeling rather scruffy, not in my best coat, and waited. He was sorting out other business, but I wanted to get home. Eventually, he was ready for off, with two other young ladies, one either side of him. They were walking home, as they lived nearer, but as we walked along this narrow path, I had to wheel my bike in the gutter.

I said,

"Would you please tell me what you want so that I can get on my bike and go home?"

He said,

"Do you mind very much walking to the road where it divides please?"

By this time I was becoming irritated but reluctantly carried on, then, as we came to the division in the road, the other two young ladies departed. He turned to me and said,

> "I want to ask you if you would like to come to the pictures with me on Monday evening."

I was flabbergasted. His name was Harold and I asked him how he knew me. He explained that he could see me taking the Brownies, from up above, when playing the organ. So that is how our romance began!

Meeting boys and making dates was not like now. Whenever I had been asked on a date previously, they usually didn't arrive. Even when they did come and I took them home, my sister Gladys was usually the one who took their fancy! So, after that first meeting with Harold when he asked me to go to the cinema with him, I thought he wouldn't turn up.

The Monday night arrived and I was ready, all in my best. I was to meet him on the main road, by the shops on Rice Lane. So I went, and it was a freezing cold evening; I waited at the bus stop for nearly half an hour but he never arrived! I was just about to go home when a bus stopped on the opposite side of the road and I could see him standing, ready to get off, all dressed up with kid gloves too. I wasn't going to let him think I had been standing waiting for him, freezing in the cold, so I turned around and almost ran up the side road which was just by the bus stop. I walked along the top, down the next road and slowly towards him.

He said to me,

> "I am so glad you haven't been standing. I am sorry I am a bit late but the vicar of St. Cyprian's called to ask me to play for the B.B. display and I couldn't just get away at that moment."

After that, we had a lovely time and he enjoyed being amongst our big family. It took a while for me to relax and realise that it was me he liked. We were always quite different, Harold and I, and while he made me more serious, I made him more frivolous. It was a good pattern for a successful life together.

We made a good team for St. George's, he arranged lots of concerts and we acted in plays; we had great times. As there were no televisions then, large crowds turned up, and people sat on windowsills and ledges. I remember a group of children pleading,

"Can the Catholics come in?"

And of course they could. Harold was also a Boys' Brigade officer at St. Cyprian's Church where he attended prior to playing the organ at St. George's.

Harold (5th from left of the officers, not in uniform on this occasion) with some members of the Boys' Brigade.

When Harold and I were enjoying all that was entailed in the Brownies' and B.B. programmes, it was a time when youth hostels were beginning to become popular. You had to map a route where you walked from one hostel to the next, within walking distance. It was a wonderful experience, learning about the countryside, having healthy exercise and getting used to reading maps.

You had to join the Y.H.A. first, then plan a route, then apply to each hostel for the nights you wished to stay. The rules were strict, one had to walk, - no wheels allowed in those days. Then you had to wait until 5pm, tea time, before being allowed in, regardless of weather conditions. You cooked all your own meals and slept in bunk beds, with the men's section at the far end of the building from the ladies'. Everyone was given a job to do after breakfast, to keep the hostel clean and enjoyable. Then you all had to be out by 9am and on your way.

Harold was familiar with this and asked if I would go with him on holiday to the Y.H.A. in Wales. Well, my mother did, reluctantly, allow me to go after being lectured! So we did go. The first night was near Mold, at Moel Famau, and then we travelled on round Clwyd. I loved it so much.

Later we were allowed to go round some of the Lake District hostels, which started a lifelong love of the Lakes for me.

Childhood Visits

Whilst we were attending Holy Trinity School, we had five weeks summer holidays. A scheme was introduced whereby the children could travel on the tramcars at reduced rates. One penny (1d) would allow us to travel on four trams, but not during the workers' hours.

So when I was about twelve years old, my friends and I had days out. We would get one tram to the Pier Head, then change and go on to another part of Liverpool, with lovely parks, such as Woolton Woods. We took sandwiches and bottles of water and lemonade powder to put in the water, and also a ball. After a couple of hours out, we would get the tram back to the Pier Head, change and then return home.

I have mentioned about going to visit my Uncle Charles, who was my mother's sister's husband. We also had Uncle George and his wife Elizabeth. Now they lived on the Wirral, which meant a trip on the boat over the Mersey, (later the underground trains were built and one could travel straight through under the Mersey), and then a bus to Hoylake.

Uncle George had a business, Bragg and Co. where he was a director, so going to his house was rather posh. We never all went together, but at times my mother would take one or two of us.

On arrival we had to be on our best behaviour and sit quietly. It was a big house near the station and not far from the sea front. I remember a huge staircase, up the middle, with picture portraits hanging on the wall each side of the stairs. They also had a maid and we could go through to her room where she had a budgerigar in a cage.

Auntie Elizabeth was a lovely, plump person and she would take us on a walk to the sea front. They had two sons, one became a professor of dentistry and the other worked in his father's office. They were a few years older than us and I always have a picture of them coming down the staircase wearing tennis whites - something we could never aspire to.

Up on the next floor there was a beautiful grand piano. In later years, when Uncle George was on his own and Harold and I visited him, when we were courting, he always asked Harold to play some of the classics, which he loved listening to.

The Joys of Life!

At this time in our lives, the talking movies had come to the cinemas! We could go to the matinees for 2d. There were two or three local cinemas, and they were packed with children on Saturday afternoons. We took an orange or some nuts. You can imagine the after effects of all that orange peel, but there were never any great problems or rudeness from the children, as their parents would punish them.

One Saturday evening, my parents decided to go to the pictures and they left Laura in charge. Now, we had a big black fireplace range in the kitchen and we had to shovel coal onto the fire to keep it going. If it had gone too low we would 'blow it up' by putting a sheet of newspaper right across the front. You had to be very careful not to let it catch alight. Sometimes this would be done deliberately to burn off the soot in the chimney if you could not afford to get the chimney sweep. This was dangerous and the flames could be seen coming out of the top of the chimney. It was also illegal and you could be fined, and so you would check first to make sure the local policeman was not around!

This Saturday night it was cold and the fire had nearly gone out so Laura put on the coal and spread the sheet of newspaper to 'blow it up' and get the fire going again. Well, suddenly this sheet of paper caught fire and Laura pushed it up the chimney with a long poker. It set all the soot in the chimney on fire and it came flowing down like red hot cinders onto the hearth.

So, we got frightened, and then my brother ran out and saw a policeman on point duty, directing the traffic. He ran up to him and told him about the fire. The policeman ran back with him and filled a bucket full of cold water; he put it under the tumbling fires and did manage to get it out.

However, my mother later had to attend court and was fined 5/- (5 shillings = 25 pence), which was quite a sum when the family only had just enough money to go round. She took a long time to recover from the shock and shame, never having had to go near a court before (or since).

When we all moved to our house in Rawcliffe Road, we were within walking distance of Aintree racecourse. By now we were teenagers, so when the course was opened up to the public on the Sunday before the Grand National, we thought it was great to walk all around the course, past the jumps, giving the 'glad eye' to the boys. It was called 'Jump Sunday', and it was a popular event, lots of people went. The tram cars were packed, dropping folk off at the terminus at the Black Bull. The main road to Aintree during those three days of racing was almost impassable.

We had such fun, we were in great high spirits, although there were no alcoholic drinks for us, and sex was never mentioned.

If by chance a single girl did get pregnant then it was considered a terrible disgrace. She was often too frightened to even tell her parents. Nine out of ten cases were sent away to a place where they delivered the baby. The girl then had to work for her keep until arrangements were made to have the baby adopted. Only then was she allowed home, even though she would be heartbroken with the loss of her baby, she often had no choice in the matter.

Of course, it was always considered to be the girl's fault; the father of the baby did not come into the equation. I know of cases where the girl lived the rest of her life remembering with sadness the child's birthday. Later, society woke to the fact that it was cruel and unnecessary to have to part with your baby. Mind you, it has gone from a time of severity to complacency now! The pendulum has swung right over.

The Tunnel

Since the Industrial Revolution, when all those renowned engineers in the 18th century like Brunel and Telford began inventing new materials and experimenting with different techniques, life has advanced at great speed. All the mills and factories moved on from the water wheel to gas driven machinery and then electric. Where a couple of men would take the place of twenty, huge strikes would take place. Really, the factory and mill owners used to use men unfairly. Education for the poor classes was only just starting and the working man had to work long, hard hours often for a mere pittance. Many could hardly keep their families from starvation, whilst the bosses made millions - they could build mansion houses and elaborate churches and live their over-indulgent lives to the full.

So now, in 1934, Liverpool decided to build a tunnel under the Mersey from the middle of the town through to Birkenhead on the Wirral. There was now a road tunnel as well as the underground railway. King George V and Queen Mary came to open it with the whole city taking part in the celebrations. Schools put on pageants in glorious colours; there were plays at the theatre and parades through the streets.

On the Sunday before the opening day the public were allowed to buy a ticket to walk through. It was a walk of several miles and buses were put on at various side tracks to take people back. Now we could travel on the electric trains through to anywhere on the Wirral in a very short time with no more thick smoke.

Liverpool has always been a great city for education and culture, not just in 2008. I know it has been laughed at, derided and the 'lingo' skitted at because, like every city, it does have a down side which leaves much to be desired. However, it has produced many famous people and lots of comedians.

Education has always been a priority with excellent grammar schools and night schools covering all types of academic subjects as well as interests and handicrafts. It has fine universities, two world-famous Cathedrals, a wonderful Town Hall, many distinguished buildings, theatres, cinemas and huge docks which were used for shipping around the world.

The Start of War

Sunday morning in September 1939, walking in from morning service, my mother said,

"War has been declared on Germany."

There had been rumblings and whispers before, but no-one took much notice. Even now we did not think it was of great importance, until we woke up to the reality of war.

We did not take much notice at first because we didn't want it to happen. When the Prime Minister, Mr Chamberlain, went to see Mr Hitler in Germany for talks it all seemed to bode well. We had been planning a trip to Blackpool Lights, with the church, but were told it had to be cancelled. Many of the older people went into shock because they remembered the thousands of husbands, sons, nephews and grandsons lost in the First World War.

Everyone had to register for ration books; then we were allowed a small ration of all the foods necessary for good health. With big families, the rations could be amalgamated and that made for a better meal to go round. Then we had just points for bedding or clothing, and it had to be adhered to. Sometimes there were channels through the black market, but it wasn't legal.

Then everyone was issued with a gas mask. We used to use ours as foot stools in the cinema! Next we all had to have an air raid shelter available nearby, for safety from bombs and shrapnel. If one had a garden, then an Anderson Shelter was dug into the ground at the bottom of the garden. Where there were no gardens, large, brick shelters were built down the roads, holding about 40 people each, where they could run when the air raid siren started.

People living near the underground stations in the centre of the city, took sleeping bags and spent the nights there, under cover.

As for me, we had an Anderson Shelter built down into the bottom of our garden to fit all seven of us. Mother put a double bed mattress over a ground sheet and a couple of stools in ours. We had to run in every time the sirens started and stayed until the 'all clear' came.

So we all had to cope with the challenges of war. At first all seemed quiet so everyone settled down again to ordinary life but then realization dawned with the sirens wailing and aeroplanes throbbing up above and people scrambling into shelters with the hope of staying alive.

We were North of Liverpool, not too far from the docks which received continual battery. If the sirens sounded whilst we were at work, various cellar shelters were available. At first we would run in right away, but as it happened continually, we got a bit blasé and waited until we could hear the throb of the German planes.

The war took a terrible toll on shipping too. One of the first ships to be torpedoed was the Athenia which was a liner carrying lots of children and their parents being evacuated to America for safety, a terrible tragedy!

Is Guinness Good for You?

During this period I carried on living as normally as possible. Harold and I began going out together, often to the cinema. I hadn't actually met his mother and family then. One Saturday afternoon Harold and I went to the Forum, a large cinema in the centre of town. It was a good film and afterwards we went back to my house. Quite to my surprise my mother said,

"I have a few bottles of Guinness in."

It was reckoned to be good for the nerves.

"If you would like a glass, have one."

It was so unusual for me to be offered beer. So I picked out a bottle and said to Harold,

"Oh! Look what we have got."

And I pointed the head of the bottle at him. Unfortunately the metal cap of the bottle was loose and it shot off. The Guinness spouted out all over the front of his shirt!

"Oh no! This is my brand new shirt!"

"Take it off and I will wash it for you."

So Harold stripped it off and I washed the shirt and hung it on the line in front of the big black range to dry. We had our tea and soon after the sirens started, so we all had to go down to the Anderson shelter at the bottom of our garden.

The house had three storeys with the kitchen built off the back, just a single storey. We had steps down from the back door of the kitchen to the garden. That evening when the air raid was on, the enemy decided to drop Molatov Baskets, like fire bombs, and they dropped a line of them down our road. They started setting light to many of the attics. If one had landed on our kitchen roof then Harold would have lost his shirt!

He was up and down the road with his mac on, helping people put the fires out. As soon as the all clear sounded I ran inside the house and tried to iron his shirt dry, but not being a fully trained housewife, I singed the front of it! I then had to wash it again to try to get the singe mark out but the sirens began once more and back it went over the range and we returned to the shelter.

It must have been midnight before the all clear sounded again so Harold had to put his shirt on, still damp. I often wondered what his mother thought when she saw it, and I hadn't even met her then!

As the Germans gained ground, we thought we had no chance. We could hear the bombs at night, whistling down on the docks. An occasional one would go astray and we would all duck down to wait and hear where it landed, how near or far a miss. It was so sad to go to work the next morning and see only half of a house left amidst the dust and rubble everywhere.

The next move was having the children evacuated away from danger zones. From Liverpool, the schools evacuated all their classes to places in Wales. It must have been a tremendous wrench both for the children being taken away from homes and familiarity and for the parents parting with them. There were, as always, a few who objected and would not conform.

Orders were next given for black-out curtains on every window. Not a glimmer of light must be seen from outside in case enemy aeroplanes could differentiate between cities and fields. The wardens, (A.R.P.), kept watch every night. All the tram cars had bluish, dimmed lights and we couldn't see who else was on the tram easily. The headlights of all vehicles were covered just enough for drivers to pick out the roads.

Following on, then came the call up of all young men from 18 years upwards, to go into the armed services. All the young women of workable age were interviewed for war work.

So, war comes to Liverpool. My brother was already in the Territorial Army. The T.A. was called up first, so Reg was soon enlisted in the Medical Corps. He became a stretcher-bearer who collected the wounded after each close conflict. He told us that they pitched large tents in which the men were treated.

Folk carried on life as best they could, in the blackout with lots of restrictions. I had been seeing Harold for about 18 months, when he came round to my house and told me he had received his call-up papers. He was 22 years old and I was 20 now. We had been partly dreading this, but partly knew that there was no choice and it had to be done if we were to fight Hitler, who we believed was in the wrong. We did not at that time know the full extent of his terrible plans. We had talked about getting engaged in the future, then the day arrived that he had to go off to Nottingham for training.

At that time, Ida had word to go for an interview. She had the choice of working in a munitions factory or to train for nursing, so she chose nursing. She started at Walton Hospital which was a good training hospital. They did eventually take some of the wounded soldiers as they were brought back from the front.

During this time I was doing sewing machine work, making eiderdowns. I must have been quite good at it as I was usually selected to work on the special samples. The factory changed to making life jackets, so I stayed there. Sometimes we would put little messages in the pockets, but I never got any replies.

Gladys was working in a shop where she continued and so life stayed at a reasonable level for just six months. Gladys' boyfriend, Bob was called up into the Medical Corps. Laura's boyfriend Allan, however, was a Jehovah's Witness and a conscientious objector. Ida didn't bother very much with boys, at that time, and was away from home, nursing.

With Reg and Ida having left home, this is when our close family unit started to fall apart.

Next Best Thing to an Organist

Harold was the organist for St George's Church where I was still Brown Owl, and so the Sunday after his call-up there was no organist! As I cycled up to church, the sidesman was at the gate, waiting for me and he said,

> "You will have to play the organ because Mr. Simmons is here to preach."

He was the vicar of all three churches, St Paul's, and Emmanuel as well as St George's. I was so frightened that I nearly turned back home. I said,

> "I have never played an organ."

He said,

> "You only need to play the hymns."

Well, I was so nervous! I did manage all right until the last hymn, after the sermon. It was a fast hymn with lots of small twiddley bits: 'All things Bright and Beautiful'. I did start off and as the congregation stood up, I went wrong and stopped. My heart was beating fast when Mr. Simmons leant over to me and said,

> "Shall we change the hymn?"

I said,

> "Yes please."

What an ordeal, never again!

E.A.Pierce June 2008

Four Weddings Within a Year

Harold and Edith – Best Man and Bridesmaid at Reg and Nell's wedding.

It seems the forces advised the soldiers when they were going home on embarkation leave, to think of getting married if they had a steady girlfriend, as it would give them a goal to fight for and satisfaction and contentment when away from home. So, Reg was married to Nell in the summer of 1940, Harold and I 'stood' for them as bridesmaid and best man. It was a lovely 'white' wedding. Then he was moved to Ireland for a while.

Laura came in and announced she was getting married in the November of 1940. Now Allan, her boyfriend, was very much against war. He would have objected to call-up, but having had a fall, he was diagnosed with renal problems during the health check, so was rejected for war service and just carried on with his own work. She also had a very special wedding day; she made most of the outfits herself.

Now, Harold had been enlisted in the Royal Ordinance Corps Regiment on his call-up. They apparently follow up the front line and pick up all the pieces, dealing with vehicles, catering and mail. After about six weeks in service, a letter arrived for me. I had been to work, come home and decided to make him a cake and send it off. As I was busy doing this, my mother said,

"There's a letter for you from Harold."

So I eagerly opened it and started to read. It said,

"Our unit is due for moving off abroad, so I will be coming home on embarkation leave for five days."

I only read that far and burst into tears. My mother said,

"What has happened? Is he alright?"

I was so upset; she took the letter off me to see what had happened to him. Then she said,

"You need to read the rest of this; he wants to marry you, by special licence, before he goes away."

So, when I read the letter and calmed down, I did finish the cake and sent it off. I did not yet have full details of when the five days embarkation leave would be, but I started making arrangements as far as I could.

For the special licence, I had to see the vicar of Emmanuel, and swear an Affidavit to verify my validity to marry Harold. I then had to sort out how many points I had for a new dress, also how many rations left to make a reasonable reception for just family and friends, no dining in hotels then!

As I have already said, Laura, my eldest sister had become a Jehovah's Witness when she had married Allan. However, we did not quite realise what it would entail. As Harold would be getting married in full military uniform, complete with rifle, we had conflicts of opinion. Allan wouldn't think of attending our wedding and refused to let Laura go.

Harold and Edith on their own wedding day, 1st December 1940

However, the day arrived; 1st December 1940, a real war wedding. I didn't manage to find a white dress but wore a very smart suit. As soon as I was ready to get into the car to go to Emmanuel, the sirens started loud and clear, warning of an air raid. We decided to ignore them and carried on. The church was quite full because a lot of the congregation from St George's had arrived. Harold's younger brother, Sydney, played the organ for us. We had a lovely service, even though we could hear planes overhead and the ack-ack banging loudly, from our guns. After the service, the all-clear sounded. We were taken for a run round in the wedding car, but instead of lovely countryside, we passed houses half standing, destruction and rubble everywhere.

Life must go on! We enjoyed a very nice meal; not as elaborate as we would have liked; with just a sponge cake to celebrate. Laura did decide to come, regardless of her husband's wishes; but when she got home, Allan had locked her out. My dad had to go back with her and sort it out, so peace within the family was restored.

We had a lovely four days together. Whenever I hear the song 'Waltzing Matilda', it reminds me of Harold and me dancing around the kitchen table in Rawcliffe Road, with that tune on the radio, on the morning he had to go back to his regiment and the war.

Then I had to go down to Lime Street Station with Harold to see him off, knowing that he would soon be abroad, in the fighting. Harold's father and my father decided to come with me. It was a very moving time. There were hundreds of soldiers, all in full uniform, with their families, about to go away. Then the orders came to leave their families and get on the train; the whistle blew to move off. Lots of the soldiers were hanging out of the windows, waving away.

As the train disappeared, Harold's dad and mine had to hold me back at the shoulders. Then the platform was left with weeping families.

I will say now that I didn't see him again for $3\frac{1}{2}$ years; but I was so glad and thanked God that he did come home eventually.

Gladys also decided to marry her boyfriend, Bob, the following June and her wedding (the fourth within the year) was a very pretty affair. However, Bob demanded that Gladys moved away with him when he was detailed to go to London. We were very concerned as it was a more dangerous war zone; the Germans had now reached France, and London was being bombed very heavily. So, she went to Staines and worked there for a while.

Early War Time

After Harold had gone abroad, I heard no more for about 3 months; then I received, by post, a package of three letters, all waterlogged and the ink had run. I thought he must have been drowned. When the embarkation ships sailed, they had to sail zigzag to avoid torpedoes and overhead bombing. Entire battalions slept in hammocks on deck, packed close. We were never told where they were going and the only kind of mail allowed was a small aerograph which was censored; any information not allowed was blotted out.

During these years of separation, lots of women had to take up men's jobs. This was one effect of the war which benefited and elevated the value of women. Pre-war, when career girls got married, they had to relinquish their jobs and stay at home to look after the man. Then they had to make do with the amount of money the husband chose to give them for housekeeping, and later for feeding and clothing the children that arrived. He could go to the pub and enjoy his beer, because it was his money and he had been working hard all week! No account taken of the skills and effort needed to run a house and bring up the children.

There were very many families just living from hand to mouth; the mother quite often struggling on because there was no alternative. It wasn't all doom and gloom though, some families found simple happiness and progressed.

So now, women could earn their own wages and please themselves how they spent it. They also became proficient at many new jobs or careers which had not been open to them before. They proved they could be as clever as men and sometimes better, and after experiencing that, never went back to full dependency on a man. Women became very independent, passed exams, went to university and even became managers and bosses.

I was now the only one still at home with my parents, but then Gladys decided that she was coming home as she was pregnant. She had a baby girl. The arrangements were that after the baby was delivered at the hospital in Liverpool, immediately, both mother and baby would be moved to Southport Maternity Hospital, away from the bombing.

So, Irene was born, and she was a delight; I was able to take her out and about quite a lot when they returned home. Also, Laura had a little girl near the same time called Anne. She too, was lovely, but I didn't see as much of her as they had their own house.

I visited Harold's mother from time to time as both her sons had left home. Harold was with the army and Syd, who was at the Collegiate Grammar School, had been evacuated to Bangor, in North Wales; she felt the draught.

I learnt after a while that Harold was in the 8th Army, under General Montgomery and with the 4th Indian Division in the Middle East. The R.O.C. worked behind the lines, moving up towards the front line, so I listened avidly to any news on the radio about the movements of the 8th Army.

The 4th Indian Division included the Ghurkhas who worked with Harold's unit.
And the saying goes,

'Two soldiers were arguing and the Ghurkha lifted his knife; the bloke he was arguing with said,

"Ha! You never touched me."

The Ghurkha said,

"You try nodding your head."'

Sweater and Helmet

I carried on sewing life jackets at the factory and I continued to go out in the blackout. If the sirens had started and I was already out, I would get back home by darting from shelter to shelter, dodging the shrapnel. It doesn't seem real now, but at the time we thought of it as normal life.

A funny thing happened one Saturday afternoon. My dad often used our big wooden table in the kitchen for making things, using his woodwork skills. The table always had a cramp fixed to one end. On this particular Saturday, my mother had gone to bed for her afternoon rest, which she often did, so dad and I were the only ones around.

To explain first, my mother had knitted dad a lovely Fair Isle sweater in different coloured patterns, for his birthday, and this he was wearing. As I have said before, he mended everything that needed to be mended.

Well, this day, he decided to try to mend our big clock; it was not quite as large as a grandfather clock. He got it down from the shelf and started to undo the screws. This clock had a very strong spring and as he pressed it against his chest to unlock the spring, his hand slipped and the spring jumped into action. It started to wind up at speed and drew in the front of his sweater. All the wool was winding round the spring and as it went in, the neck of his jumper was being pulled down, tighter and tighter. I took one look, (I must say that I was noted for being a giggler), I just sat on the chair, almost hysterical, laughing.

He was shouting,

"Help me, I'm choking!"

But the neck was pulling away from his throat.

He said,

"Stop your bloody laughing and help me!"

I couldn't see how I could undo this clock, so I got the scissors and cut it off, which left a huge, roughly circular hole in the front of his sweater! He took it off and looked at it and said to me,

"Can you mend it?"

Well, that set me off laughing again. How could anyone mend an enormous hole in the middle of a patterned sweater?
He said,

"What can I say to your mother? She will go mad."

So, he rolled it up and put it in the back of his wardrobe. I never heard how it ended when mum found it months later. Life will always have a funny side!

Another time, dad was getting ready to go on air raid warden duty. There was a duty rota when one had to go outside and watch for any chinks of light from houses or for incendiary bombs (Molotov Baskets). Sometimes these poured down from the enemy planes, setting fire through roofs. We all had to help to put them out; we did have some training at the fire station.

Well, he went into the hall to get his coat and helmet, which was high up on a hook. As he reached up, the metal helmet crashed down on his forehead and made a big gash over his eye. He came staggering in, holding his head, with the blood pouring down. I took one look and again burst out laughing!

However, I did eventually calm down, bathed it for him and put a plaster on. We always managed with home remedies then – we never thought of running to the hospital.

Gone with the Wind

When the film 'Gone with the Wind' was released, it was going to be on at the Forum, a big cinema in the middle of town. I said that I would go down and book the tickets for all those who wanted to go, about twelve of us, mostly family. I duly booked these tickets and they all paid me, then we waited a couple of weeks, looking forward to the great day.

On the Wednesday before, Reg and Nell called in and after a chat and coffee, they decided to take their two tickets and we would meet them in the foyer.

Well, the day before the event, as I was about to set off for work, I checked to make sure all was OK. I couldn't find the tickets where I thought I had put them. I started to search and search with no luck. I didn't get to work and had to ring the Forum to say that I had lost the tickets. They told us to come down anyway, and stand in the foyer. I had to ring everyone else up and confess, so then we did all meet in the foyer before the start of the film.

With all the crowds milling around, we could hardly stand up and we had to wait until the film was about to start until an usherette came to lead us up five lots of stairs to the 'gods'. Gladys was with me and it was only a few weeks after her baby was born; she started to feel sick and the group were annoyed. I had to take Gladys outside after a while so we didn't see it all.

You can imagine how I felt. I don't think I followed the story of 'Gone with the Wind' at all and I never found those tickets.

I watched it on TV recently and, my goodness, that took me back!

Exmouth

We valued having moonlit nights as we could see our way around, but so could the enemy! During that time, Gladys had little Irene, who was now walking. Her husband, Bob, was moved down to Exmouth with the medics and insisted that she go and join him, which she did. After about 8 months, I re-

ceived a letter from Glad, asking if I would come down since Bob had suffered a nervous breakdown and had been taken to hospital.
There had been quite a rumpus, with the police involved, so feeling rather worried; my mother said that I should go.

I rose early the next morning, got the tram to Lime Street Station and caught, as I thought, the appropriate train. It was a very long journey and I was on my own, in the blackout. After about six hours, the train stopped at Exeter and I got off. When I came out of the station, it was late and going twilight. I approached a policeman and asked him the way to this address I had written down. He said,

> "It's Exmouth you want, not Exeter. You will have to go to that bus terminus and there will be a bus to take you there."

I had no idea there were two different places. So, I duly waited in a small queue for about 20 minutes and boarded the bus; it was now nearly dark. I asked the bus driver to tell me when to get off. The bus went along miles of country lanes and all I could see were trees flashing past. The lights in the bus were so dim that I could hardly see who I was sitting by. Another hour passed and I thought he had forgotten me. Eventually, he called out that it was my stop, by a library.

I stood on the pavement, in the pitch dark. All I could distinguish were the silhouettes of roofs and chimney pots. I started walking slowly along, wondering who I could ask for the way to this address. There were lots of French soldiers about and I was getting a bit anxious when I heard a lady approach. Fortunately, she was able to tell me that it was two roads further up and then turn left. I followed the lines of the rooftops and at last arrived at Glad's address. You can get anywhere with an English tongue in your head!

By now, it was midnight! I knocked and knocked; they had all gone to bed. Gladys was in an apartment but eventually opened the door and nearly collapsed when she saw me. She had been to the Exmouth train station earlier and I wasn't on that train, so had decided that I wasn't coming. Of course I had got off at the wrong station and had travelled the rest of the way by bus. She had booked me in at a bed and breakfast, down the road, so we then had to knock them up. I did relax at last, had a nice drink and fell into bed. I stayed in Exmouth for 4 days, then came home with Gladys and Irene; a great relief.

Back to Liverpool and we lived life as calmly as we could. The docks were bombed relentlessly. Street shelters were bombed, factories and warehouses; there was destruction everywhere.

The soldiers in the desert received snippets of news from England and thought some of their families must have been bombed out or killed, and lots were. Then the news began to sound a little better with the advancement of our troops across the desert then over to Italy.

The Prime Minister Mr. Churchill was a great war veteran. He would come on the radio, keeping everyone's spirits up. He would never accept defeat and insisted on battling on, so we all did battle on and put up with the hardships and losses without complaint.

Hero's Return

Now, more than three years had passed since Harold had gone away and I went to work, as usual. Ida had a couple of days' leave at home from the hospital where she worked. She rang me up at work, which was most unusual, and said,

> "There's a letter arrived this morning for you, with an English stamp and postmark, from Harold."

I asked the manager if I could go home, and permission was granted. I read his letter, but he still could not tell me much, only to say,

> "You will realise that we are in England."

When would he arrive? I needed to get everything ready! After I had cleaned the house, I took a bath and washed my hair to make myself as pretty as possible. We had a large bay window in the front parlour and I sat there all evening, wondering how he would look and what he would think of me.

It got to 11pm and still no sign of Harold. Then I went off to bed, disappointed, to say the least. What I had forgotten was that he was still in the forces and had to wait to be granted leave. I did get another letter the next day to say that he would be home as soon as he was allowed some leave.

Eventually the day arrived. He had rung me and made arrangements to meet - his train would arrive at Lime Street Station at 3pm on this Saturday in April in 1944. So Harold's mother and I planned to go down to meet him off the train. I decided to get all the work in the house done and then bathe and get dressed in my best clothes. I was just finishing off by brushing the stairs down, still in my old working clothes and pinny, when there was a knock on the front door. My mother said,

"That will be my insurance man."

Then she started to look for her purse to pay him, so I went to open the front door.

Well, well, well! Guess what! There was Harold, standing there in full army uniform, complete with three stripes, as he was now a sergeant. He looked thin and dark brown, from living in the desert all these years. He didn't seem to mind that I was in my work outfit.

We had tears and kisses and all chatted for so long. After tea, I said,

"Would you like to go to the theatre?"

So off we went, but Harold couldn't stand being closed in. He spent most of the time fanning himself; but still enjoyed it.

Not having had any honeymoon after our wedding, three and a half years previously, we decided to go to Wales together for five days. We didn't need to pre-book then, so we went off to Abergele and stayed in a guest house. The weather was so cold; it snowed most of the time. It was blowing horizontally across more than down. However, we went to the jewellers and he bought me a lovely diamond ring. We ended up every evening going to the local cinema to keep out of the cold.

After we got back home, we realised the real reason for his return to England; great plans were in place for a massive spearhead attack on France. Harold was a fully trained and experienced soldier, a sergeant, and he was one of thousands who had been ordered back to take a lead part in that move. Harold went back to his unit, to do his duty.

Every available ship, large and small was assembled and filled with soldiers. All the aircraft were prepared to give cover to the soldiers as they left the boats, landed at the coast and started to fight. Lots of airmen and other forces had already been dropped into France, secretly, some nights before in order to blow up vital works and enemy strongholds. It was to be a tremendous onslaught and very dangerous for all taking part.

We knew of it later as the D-Day Landings.

Arthur Gosby Pierce

Harold's father, Arthur Gosby Pierce, was then 51 years old. He was a member of the Home Guard (Dad's Army) as well as working in business during the day. He was walking to work one morning when he collapsed and suffered a massive heart attack. Although a passer-by called for an ambulance, sadly, he died. It was such a shock. We had to send for Harold, who had only been back in the country for about two weeks, and he was granted 10 days compassionate leave. We also had to send for Sydney, his younger brother, who had been evacuated to Bangor.

Harold came home and took over all the necessary arrangements for the funeral. His mother was now alone, but after the funeral Harold had to go back to his barracks, in Preston.

He left on the Sunday at teatime; but at about 10pm that evening, we received a phone call from Harold. He had arrived back safely to find the barracks deserted. It was quite eerie. None of his fellow men were there, but he did find an officer who explained that all the battalion had moved to the front.
Then Harold asked,

"What will I do?"

He said,

"You will have to stay here. You will never catch up to or find your regiment now."

So, Harold stayed at Preston, training new recruits, until he was demobilised a couple of years later.

This was to be the start of the end of the war, but many thousands of men did lose their lives during the Normandy landings. Harold always maintained that his father had died instead of him.

A New Family

Whilst Harold was stationed at Preston, I could go up at the weekends, if he was off duty. I stayed at one of the houses belonging to the forces that took in lodgers. We could go to the dances at the British Enca, where all the nylons were made. However, the war was still raging right across France. Much to our relief, we were making great progress, according to the news.

Eventually the great day arrived in 1945, V.E. Day, victory in Europe. What a marvellous time we had, dancing in the streets, ships hooters blowing, church bells ringing; merrymaking and peace.

But all was not completely over. The war in the Pacific still raged on until America decided to use those horrific nuclear bombs on Japan. They were dropped on Hiroshima and Nagasaki and they had far reaching and long lasting effects.

It certainly put an end to war and we could get back to normal living.

In October 1945, we were thrilled at the arrival of our first baby, a lovely daughter, Marjorie. When Harold came to the hospital on the evening she was born, he picked her up and said,

"Yes, just like me, no teeth!"

Of course Harold had had full dentures since the age of 21, as was quite common then. As he was still in the forces, he was only allowed a short spell at home.

In our day, we had to stay in hospital, in bed, for two weeks after delivering a baby, then back home where a nurse visited every day for another week. So, I came home with Marjorie, a very proud new mum.

I was only home a week when both mum and dad took ill with a very bad type of flu, so had to stay in bed. I was now the only one of our family of five still living at home. Laura, Reg and Gladys each had their own council house with children growing up and Ida lived at the hospital, now S.R.N. status.

We lived in a large house, with no central heating and it was November, so very cold. I had to nurse both of them, carrying coal for their fire up from the cellar to the bedroom, make all the meals, clean the house and care for my new baby. I had a nice high pram I could cuddle her up in and rock, but I was so scared of her catching this flu. I didn't dare take her up to their bedroom. However, these things don't last for ever and all went well.

Harold was demobilised in1946, receiving a £32 gratuity, a suit of clothes and a pair of shoes. He was awarded some medals which he had thoroughly earned, but not even a thank you letter. Fortunately, he did get back to the job he had left six years previously.

War from Post War Perspective

It wasn't until the men started to arrive home that we learnt some of the truth; but many of them did not want to talk much about it, and Harold was always very reluctant to go into serious detail.

Whilst the armies had been advancing and retreating across the desert near Tunisia and Tripoli during the worst bombardments, the men on the ground had to dig holes, deep in the sand, with just a bivouac over the hole for cover and camouflage. At that time, Harold was driving huge wagons and was often faced with terrible conditions such as sandstorms. The wagons would get bogged down and had to be dug out by hand. There were lulls between the fighting, from time to time, when the wounded soldiers were picked up. The enemy soldiers were also rounded up and sent to prison camps or prison hospitals depending on what shape they were in.

Some of the families never really knew if their loved ones were in prison camps or dead. You see, at home, if a soldier was missing, it was the system for a young man, a telegraph boy on a bike, to deliver a telegram from the War Office to his home. This gave his name and 'missing, presumed dead'. And that was it! No follow up; no counselling; just that. So whenever we saw a telegraph boy coming up the road on his bike, we waited and watched which house he was going to, holding our breath; it could be anyone.

The soldiers who were sent to the Far East had some terrible experiences. They had to go through swamps and were covered in leeches. One of Reg's brothers-in-law was in a prisoner of war camp in Burma. His wife thought he was dead, having received a telegram. However, a short time after the war was over, he arrived home in a terrible state.

The treatment in the prison camps was bad, as we now know through the films, which are not exaggerated. Very occasionally a couple of P.O.W.'s would try to break out, but if caught were immediately shot. We did hear of their terrible plight from the one or two who made it home.

I had a friend, Maisie, whose husband, John, was in the R.A.F. He was a rear gunner and when they went on a mission one night, the plane was shot down in Germany. The procedure was, if possible, to dig a hole and bury the parachute and kit, then find your way to the nearest church and hide. The churches were always open. In most countries, there were underground workers and these very brave people would risk being shot and follow up air crashes to seek out the hiding places. So, John was lucky. He and his friend were taken to a farm.

The airmen were given a change of clothes and taken to a safe place to hide out until a way could be found to get them home. If the Germans got wind of anything, they sent out search parties. Word did get out and the underground workers had to hide them in a hay cart, where they lay for two whole days. They could hear the Germans in the background. When all was clear again, they brought a couple of bikes, as there were two of them, dressed them in local clothes and told them not to speak to anyone. They were given a route to take, which went over the mountains, and were told to meet at a particular train station where transport would take them across the border to a neutral zone and safety.

John survived and lived to a good age with Maisie and their family. He said it was the most terrifying experience, riding that bike in enemy country.

Whilst abroad, the army divisions were sometimes granted leave, but only locally. They went in small groups, perhaps to the capital city for a week or ten days holiday. All the time they had to keep in touch with their unit to follow their position, because of getting back to the right spot. Sometimes it was very difficult finding exactly the right area, the movement of the front line being so continual. Another hazard experienced by the men was infestation of fleas or lice. Before going on any of the holidays they had to take most of their clothes and uniform to a point where they were put into machines for sterilisation and delousing. The flies also got into everything. It was an experience that just had to be endured.

Post War Britain

The next move, now that the war was really over, was getting back to work, for the able ones. We were very lucky in that Harold still had his job open for him. He had served his time at Perrin Hughes Builders' and Plumbers' Merchants in Liverpool before the war, and, as was the practice then, he was understudying the Estimate Clerk, so that when he retired, Harold would carry on.

Harold's mother, Gladys Pierce, lived on her own now as Syd had gone to sea with the 'Alfred Holt Line', training to be a ship's engineer. He eventually became a Master Marine Engineer and emigrated to Hong Kong.

I didn't go back to work. The jersey embroidery business had stopped during the war and now it started to filter back. However, the designs were now much simpler, just 'CUNARD', no elaboration. I carried on doing it with my mother. If a large order arrived then my sisters would help out, as they lived not far away, one in Aintree and the other in Fazakerley.

Ida now decided she was going off to Sheffield to train for midwifery, which she enjoyed doing. She became a midwife in Handsworth in Sheffield and rented a large house there. It turned out to be very beneficial to us as we could then go on holidays to Yorkshire. It was a new innovation for us to be able to travel freely to other parts of the country. Bus travel had become more common, instead of trams. We could get into

Liverpool easily on the bus, then the train through the Woodhead Tunnel, but rarely went further afield.

It was quite exciting. There were no toilets on trains then, so one had to get out when the train stopped at a convenient station. You had to be quick and back on board before the whistle blew for the driver to set off again. There were clouds of thick smoke belching out; a sight to see; then the hooter would blow as we gathered speed.

As well as the trains being smoky, every house had a coal fire so that there was thick smoke rising out of every chimney pot. No wonder we had fog and smog. It was mainly in the winter when the clouds were low. You could hardly find your way home through the thick smog in Liverpool. It wasn't good for asthmatics, and any washing hanging on the line was soiled with sooty smuts.

While Ida was living in Sheffield, we took the opportunity to take days out around Derbyshire, visiting the caves near Castleton, Matlock and The Lady Bower Dam. We still had our rucksacks and Harold's had a strong frame, so we hiked along with Marjorie standing in the rucksack. In time, both Joyce and Jeannette our other two children, had their turn.

Now we were a family, but still living in Rawcliffe Road with my mum and dad, so we decided to try for a corporation house. So we went to the Town Hall, to the housing department, but since everything in that line had stood still while the war was on, it was extremely hard to even make the waiting list. You acquired points according to your circumstances.

An officer came to assess our situation in Rawcliffe Road. It was a big house; he took one look and as there was plenty of room to accommodate all of us, he decided that we had no points and no chance of a council house. I was very disappointed as I would have dearly loved my own home, and there was no way we could afford to buy one. So that was where we stayed. It was a nice neighbourhood and eventually we agreed to splitting the rooms so that we could have our own space as a family.

Life went on. Harold was back to work at Perrin Hughes. My brother and sisters, with their families visited us and vice versa. Laura still had only Anne. Reg and Nell had four children, Dorothy, Brenda, Kenneth and Norman. Gladys's family eventually grew to five, Irene, Brian, Ian and later on Hilary and Gordon. We had our three daughters, Marjorie, Joyce and Jeannette. We were now quite a big family.

Mad Dog and Ankle

I recall one of the holidays at Ida's in Sheffield, when we had only Marjorie and Ida had a dog. It had been the last of the litter, a spaniel, and it must have been a bit stupid because whenever it was taken outside it would keep running away. It was very difficult to make it come back – really it was a bit of a pest. However, one day, when Ida was out on a case, I decided to take this dog for a walk on the lead with Marjorie in the go-chair. We were having a good walk when I stopped to fix a strap on the pram and as I did so the dog pulled and the lead shot out of my hand. It was near a main road; I was horrified. It was hopeless trying to catch her, so I went back to Ida's home.

Just as I arrived, Ida returned for a snack before going back to the woman nearer the time for delivery of her baby. Well, I had to tell her that the dog had run away. She said not to worry and that it would find its way back again. By now it was time for her to get back for the birth and for Marjorie to go to sleep. After I had put her in bed and read a story, I went down and could hear the dog barking in the back garden. I decided to try to catch her because I felt responsible for losing her, and if I could just get my foot on the lead then I could grab her.

The gardens at the back slanted upwards, then a step onto a plateau with trees at the far side along the top. It was now very dark but I thought I was so near to catching the dog that I chased after her. After a few yards, I felt myself falling off this plateau and landing on the ground below, between two bins with my leg twisted under me. I couldn't believe what had happened. I was in so much pain that I could hardly get up, but I had to, and so dragged my leg all around the side to the main road and back to Ida's. Just at that moment she arrived back from her case and was aghast at what she saw. I was feeling faint so she rang the hospital and I had to go and have it x-rayed. Luckily it wasn't broken, but badly bruised and strained, so I had to stay another three weeks at Ida's until I could walk on it.

Harold came at the weekend and helped me round to show me where I had fallen. I was amazed to see where I had dropped. It was a six foot wall I had walked off.

My leg has never been quite right since then, but I can't say that it has ever held me back.

Kenneth

We now were living at a steady pace for a while when my brother arrived at the house. Nell, his wife, had just had Norman, their youngest son. She had been having trouble with her teeth, so, as was popular then, suddenly decided to have all her teeth out. It was the usual practice then to have teeth taken out if you had toothache rather than fillings.

Marjorie and Kenneth in the back garden at Rawcliffe Road

Unfortunately, Nell ended up in hospital with a nervous breakdown. Now we realise that the shock of having a mouthful of teeth out at once can cause a nervous reaction. Well, they had two daughters, Dorothy and Brenda, then Kenneth who was two years old as well as the new baby, Norman. Nell's mother took the baby and the girls to look after and I said that I would have Kenneth.

I was still living with my parents. Marjorie was quite delighted to have Kenneth as a play pal. So we looked after him for about 6 months; he was part of our family and we took him everywhere, even on holiday to Abergele for a week. Eventually Nell was well enough to cope and he went back home.

When we were first living in Rawcliffe Road and involved with the Brownies and Guides we learnt that one of the Guides had lived with her family some years before in the exact same house, where we were now living.

The Greenhalgh family lived a big, fully detached house in Grey Road on the next corner further up Rawcliffe Road. This family consisted of the Grandmother, twin daughters of about 40 years who always dressed alike, another daughter and a son. The daughter had two boys of about 10 and 12. I remember them walking past our house, well dressed in college uniforms.

The son was seafaring and he got married to a relation of the people who had previously lived in our house. They had three children but being seafaring, he was away a great deal. I became quite friendly with his wife, as we took the children back and forth to school, since their house was nearby. An opportunity came for her to join him and take a holiday flying to Paris – very adventurous for those days. She was a bit nervous of leaving the children for the first time, but it was arranged that they were to stay with a neighbour.

There was a terrible tragedy and the plane crashed; both parents were killed. So, the three children went to live with their aunt and she then brought them up. They sometimes stayed with their grandmother in Grey Road. One of the girls, Elizabeth, was Marjorie's age and they often played together.

Several years later, after Kenneth's sister Brenda died, he was very traumatised and became an atheist and confronted the minister at the funeral. The minister decided to get to know Kenneth and talk to him to try to help. He called at Reg's a number of times and Kenneth started to listen to him and eventually joined the church. It was an evangelical church with a good youth following. Now, Kenneth knew nothing at all about Rawcliffe Road and the story I have just written but, a couple of years later, Reg rang me telling me that Kenneth had met a nice girl and was getting engaged. When he told me her name, how amazing! It was Elizabeth Greenhalgh. Yes, one of the orphaned children!

What is even more amazing is that Kenneth trained and became a pastor of the church. Kenneth and Elizabeth are still happily married with two children and grandchildren of their own.

A rather sad and strange incident took place a while later when the grandmother of the people who had previously lived in our house, (I can't quite recall if this would be Elizabeth's other grandmother), came knocking on the door looking for her husband. She had become old and started with Alzheimer's disease, so was confused and thought that she still lived there. I asked her in and then took her home later on.

The Middle One

Marjorie at $4\frac{1}{2}$ years old, was quite a bright child; her dad often took her out and taught her the names of places and bits of history. I sometimes learned new things myself listening to them. She was the apple of her dad's eye. I was then delighted to find I was expecting my second child. The time came round, and she too was a little dream named Joyce. Her first year passed without many incidents, but when she started to walk she was off and into everything!

At 19 months old, Joyce was playing at the foot of the stairs when she slipped and caught her arm in the banister. I thought it was OK at first, but when I came to wash her, before bed, she screamed as I lifted her arm. Harold and I carried her down to Walton Hospital, a good mile away.

When we first arrived a nurse put two spatulas or splints on and bandaged it up until we saw the doctor and had it x-rayed. We waited so long that she had pulled those spatulas out and was hitting us and the chairs with them. Eventually the verdict was a double greenstick fracture. We then had a further wait until she was admitted to theatre and had it set.

When we came home she had a big plaster cast but that didn't stop her walking about. I thought she would break the other arm with all the climbing on chairs she tried. One tea time after she had finished eating, she was standing by a chair and I had a terrible shock when I thought I saw her arm shoot off across the table! Fortunately, it was only the plaster cast; she must have caught it on the edge of the chair. We had to dash back to the hospital for them to put a fresh cast on.

We didn't know it at the time but that became the first of many visits to hospital with Joyce.

Roof Repairs

The house we were living in, in Rawcliffe Road, was about 90 years old and was having a few problems regards repairs. We were renting it so had to inform the landlord if building work was necessary. It was a three storey house with large bay windows. One of the back bedroom ceilings started leaking so some workmen eventually arrived to mend the bay roof. They had borrowed a bucket and brush from us at the start, for the cement, and they seemed to be taking a long time on the roof. At dinner time I had to go down the road for some shopping with the children and the pram. As I came out of the front door and down the steps, I heard the workmen up on the front bay roof. I called up to them and asked,

> "Why are you on the front bay?"

Quite glibly they replied,

> "I am sorry, we dropped a ridge tile and it caused a crack which we are mending."

I went on my way, believing them. When I returned, they had finished, packed up and gone; bucket and brush too. When my dad came home from work, I told him the story and he immediately went up the stairs, opened the bay window and put a chair out to stand on. My dad was always quite agile and had a good knowledge of buildings. The bay roof sloped quite a bit but he stood on the chair, holding on to the roof gutter. I was terrified that he would fall.

He was on his toes, stretching up, looking over the roof and said,

> "The buggers have taken all the lead flashings!"

Lead was at a premium, and it had to be reported to the police. It ruined the roof, and when the rain came, it poured down the walls inside, so more workmen came to repair it, but didn't replace it with lead. It held for a while, but it was never the same. The police did catch up with them about six months later, doing another house.

A Right Royal 'Do'

Before the war broke out our king, George V started having problems with ill health. I was at the Guides' hall at Holy Trinity when news came in that he had died, and there was to be a huge royal funeral.

As soon as a monarch dies, the heir to the throne is named, announcing the new king or queen and proclaiming "Long live the King! (or Queen)". At that time, the heir was Edward, the eldest son. At first it seemed OK, but as he was involved with a twice-divorced lady, Mrs. Simpson, he had to choose her or the throne. So after long searching and thought, Edward decided to abdicate. I can still see the large print on all the papers –

"EDWARD ABDICATES"

It did cause a great stir.

Then his brother, who became George instead of Bertie, had to pick up the reins. He was then married to Elizabeth, and had two daughters, Elizabeth and Margaret. So the coronation was for George VI. His wife was a great support, and the eldest daughter Elizabeth had to train for the throne. The girls were now reaching late teens, and dating. Their names and pictures were printed on tins of toffee, boxes of chocolates, and lots of other products.

The Royal Family carried on valiantly during the war years, although part of one of the palaces was damaged through bombing.

In the late 1940's Ida was training to be a midwifery tutor, living in Sheffield. During those years, my mother would stay with her for quite long periods. Dad would go to be with her at the weekends, but he would have to return to Liverpool to go to work during the week.

We had nice social times when the families visited. Occasionally we fell out over differences, or the children doing something that upset someone, but it passed over, as in most families.

The salient news, on the radio at this time, was the romance of Princess Elizabeth and Prince Philip. There were doubts at first, and then came the announcement of the Wedding Day. Not many people had televisions yet – we certainly didn't. They were starting to be available, and the early ones were only black and white of course. It was still an exciting time, and a great day for the Royal Family.

Following that, of course, was the birth of Prince Charles, born on my mother's birthday, 14th November. A couple of years later came the birth of Princess Anne. Then came the sad news of King George's failing health. It was when Elizabeth and Philip were on holiday in Africa, in a tree top safari park, that they received the news that her father had died.

They had to return home immediately, because she was heir to the throne. It was a sad time, because he was dearly loved. When the period of mourning was over, all the preparations for the coronation had to take precedence.

By now, my cousins Millie and Frank had bought a television set. Frank was a merchant seaman, so was fairly well off. All our families made arrangements to go to their house, to watch this coronation. We all took different food to share, and it was really exciting.
It took hours to watch all the procedures that had to be followed. The next day, nearly every street had a party; families had parties; everyone had parties. There were flags with red white and blue, cakes with crowns on, and great merry-making.

Following the coronation was more news of great importance: Sir Edmond Hilary and Sherpa Tensing had successfully climbed Mount Everest for the first time.

The Isle of Man

One of the best holidays we had was when the children were quite young, in fact before Jeannette was born and long before people flew on aeroplanes for their holidays. Harold and I decided we would take a special holiday across the sea to the Isle of Man. I remember Harold's brother when he was young and they went to the Isle of Man on holiday. He proudly declared,

"It's the first time I have been out of England."

It was a four hour sea journey in a large ferry boat. Marjorie would be about 8 years and Joyce $3\frac{1}{2}$. Now this was something different, the Isle of Man was like a beautiful jewel in the Irish Sea off the West coast of England, opposite Blackpool.

It was exciting going up the gang plank then watching the ropes being released. I think the boat was called the 'Manx Maid'. Harold and the girls were exploring all over the boat and he was explaining all about the buildings we could see disappearing from view.

Now I was never good at travelling long distances and as we journeyed on, I began to feel sea-sick. As we were nearing the Isle of Man, the children were saying,

"Come on mum, we can see it".

We didn't have travel tablets then and by now I dared not move for fear of being sick!

This holiday was at Cunningham's Holiday Camp near Douglas. It was the first time we had ever been on that type of holiday. A man called 'Butlin' had started setting up camps at different seaside areas and they became very popular with continual entertainment for all the family.

There were chalets for the families to live in and paths from the wooden chalets to the very large dining room with lots of long tables, all numbered. On arrival we were given a key with the chalet number and our table for meals. There were lots of loudspeakers and workers in yellow aprons. We were also told the times of our meals. They had everything we needed for entertainment for the young ones, the older ones and for children, all separate.

After we had unpacked in our chalet we still had a couple of hours to go before our meal time so we decided to go in the swimming pool. I still felt very sick and had a terrible headache but when I came out of that pool I felt wonderful and ready to go.

After our tea we walked around the camp finding the way to different rooms for entertainment. The children had games with clowns and magicians and there were lots of competitions. People who had children could put them to bed and tell one of the wardens who would come round checking to see that all was well, while the parents went down to the dance hall. We did mainly ballroom dancing, which was great. If any problems arose, it would be announced over the loud speakers, calling your name to return to your chalet.

On the Sunday after breakfast, visitors from all over the island went to the open-air service at Kirk Braddan. It was awe-inspiring joining with so many and singing hymns in the open with beautiful scenery all around. We sat on tree trunks or the grass. In the afternoon there was a Sunday School for the children down on the sands, followed by a competition for who could build the best sand castle. I don't remember much rain.

On the Monday we had a coach trip out to Snaefel and on the route we had to stop in one of the glens so that all the children could say 'Good Morning' to the fairies.

'No More Strikes'

During the week we were asked to make fancy dresses for the children's party on the Friday. I bought some black crepe paper and made a workman's suit for Marjorie. I stuck dead matches all over it and made a sign saying 'NO MORE STRIKES'. For Joyce, I made a pixie outfit out of green crepe paper with wings and little bootees. She says that she can only remember how slippery it was trying to walk across the floor with crepe paper shoes.

On the Friday evening, they had a lovely concert on a huge stage with the children all in fancy dress. The room was packed with lots of families. Marjorie did get first prize and I also remember her playing 'Greensleeves' on an enormous grand piano. What a clap she got!

On Thursday we went to Laxey to see the huge wheel all painted in pretty colours. Harold took the girls up lots of steps to the top and they were waving down to me. During that holiday, we met another family, same as us, and we had a lovely time dancing to Glen Ross and his band most evenings. A holiday to remember!

We did return another year to the same camp, but it wasn't quite as good as that first time.

Family of Three

It was now 1954, and my third daughter Jeannette was born. The same day, Harold's brother Sydney was expected home from Hong Kong. He was a ship's engineer. So his mum was all agog waiting for both to arrive! Jeannette was another little dream, a bigger baby, and very contented.

Marjorie was now reaching the age to sit the "Eleven-plus" scholarship exam. She was usually placed within the top group in her class. The school had been having an internal test that particular day, and she came home and showed me her results from the test. They placed her way down in class. My reaction was to shout at her, being surprised at the poor result so near to the scholarship exam. While I was cross she said,

> "I have a headache!"

Then she started to be sick. She felt very hot, so I took her to the doctors. The doctor said,

> "Take her home and prepare her for the hospital. I have sent for an ambulance; she has appendicitis."

I was so mortified and sorry at being cross over school work! All the way in the ambulance I apologised for being cross, and told her it didn't matter about school work, so long as she got better!

She did; and, I must add, she passed the scholarship!

When we were filling in the forms for the scholarship, we had to decide which school would be best to apply for. Harold and I thought the nearest, with no big main roads to cross, would be best, but Marjorie herself dearly wanted to go to Holly Lodge.

This meant two buses to take, and two main roads to cross! Our precious child's first venture!
However, we had to attend a parents' evening before the exams, and when we spoke with the teachers, they gave us quite a glowing account of Marjorie's abilities. So we did give in, and to Holly Lodge she went.

No parents allowed near on the first morning! I anxiously awaited her return straight after school, but guess what! No sign of Marjorie! I am now in a spin – where is she??? At 5pm she came casually walking up the street. She had only stayed back to join the Christian Union, and had enjoyed her day!

A family of three

Operations

Not long after this, Joyce, my middle daughter, started with the measles. She had always been a bit 'chesty', and although she recovered quite well from the measles, her chest continued to sound very rattley.

One day, when Ida was home for a weekend, I was bathing Joyce and I said to Ida,

> "I am a bit worried about Joyce. Listen to her chest!"

> "Take her to the doctors," said Ida.

> "I have, and she tells me I fuss too much."

> "Then take her to one of the mobile units, they x-ray anyone who calls in."

So that's what I did. They told me that if anything was wrong, I would hear within ten days. I waited, and waited, then on the tenth day, I had a letter to go back for a deeper x-ray. So of course we went, and the diagnosis was a bronchiectasis.

This started a long follow-up of hospital treatment. Joyce was in and out of hospital trying different therapies. At last we had an appointment to see the hospital consultant, and he told me,

> "As this bronchiectasis is localised, we can now operate, and take out the lower section of the lung."

When Ida had started nursing, operating on lungs was unheard of. Even at that time it was very much in its infancy. To Harold and me it was a frightening thought to decide upon. Ida said,

> "Be guided by the consultant. He knows his job."

So we did agree to the operation. Joyce, now seven years old, was admitted to hospital. There were no antibiotics then, so she was kept in three weeks before the operation, to make sure the blood count was right. Then there was a procedure to paint the body pink from shoulder to tummy the night before the operation. Each night she would say,

> "I've washed myself down to my middle so they can paint me."

It used to make me shudder with anxiety.

Joyce had been in the hospital for two weeks. As she was in a special ward, the others were all adults. Then another little girl from Wales was admitted with the same complaint. They kept each other company, and played together.

During all this time, Harold's mother was very good. She did a lot of baby minding and ironing for me. She would say,

> "God must think I think he's deaf, as I'm praying and praying all the time!"

Now it was nearing the day for the operation, and I went at visiting time as usual (two buses there, and two buses back). As I walked down the ward, I saw the other little girl's bed was empty. I asked Joyce,

> "Where is your little friend?"

Just at that moment, the Sister called me into her office, and asked me,

> "Has Joyce ever had Chicken Pox?"

> "No," I answered.

> "The other little girl has gone home with Chicken Pox. You will have to take Joyce home in case she has caught the germs. This is a surgical ward, and we have to be so careful."

So I dressed Joyce and rang for a taxi to take her home again. You may be sure I was so upset. She was saying,

> "What are you crying for, Mummy? I am coming home!"

It was so hard to be so near to facing her having the operation, and now to be back to square one again! However, she did get the Chicken Pox. So did Jeannette, the baby. So did Marjorie – she took it the worst.

I look back on one evening, when all three had Chicken Pox. I had put them all to bed, and Joyce woke up crying, saying she felt ill. Jeannette woke up and started crying, then Marjorie, who was in a separate bedroom, started crying and said she was crying because the others were, so she also felt miserable! To cap it all, it was thundering and lightening outside, and Harold had had to go to see to something at church, so I was on my own! I didn't know which one to go to first, so I sat on the top of the stairs and stared crying myself!

Two days after, it was Jeannette's 3rd birthday, so we had a 'spotty party' with everyone with Chicken Pox, which we have all laughed about since.

Of course, all was not over yet, and we had to wait until Joyce's blood count was right again before going back into hospital. Time, as always, passes, and she was readmitted. Once again it was a three week wait.

During those weeks, my sister Gladys came with me on day time visiting. We were allowed half an hour only and then promptly ushered out again. Two days before the operation we had a phone call from Gladys's family. She had been taken into another hospital, and was having her gall bladder removed the very same day as Joyce's operation. So my mother and I both had our daughters in theatre together, and we waited and waited. At 3pm, we went up to the main road to find a phone to ring up, to see how they were. They told me Joyce was still in theatre, so I went back home, worried out of my mind.

Sometimes life dishes out some very odd coincidences!

It was getting time to go back up to the phone, to see if we could find out how Joyce was, when there was a knock on the front door. Harold was just home from work. We had a glass-framed front door, and through it we could see two men in uniform. We guessed it must be the police from the hospital. As Harold looked, he pushed me back in and said,

"I will deal with this."

Then he opened the door. It was two Boys' Brigade officers, who had come to ask him to play the music for their display! How ironical – but what a great relief to us!

Thankfully, both Joyce and Gladys eventually came home lots better.

The Great Fire

At this time, we still lived in Rawcliffe Road, which was a lovely large house, but getting rather old. Ida had arrived home for the weekend, and we had Mum, Dad, Harold and I, Marjorie, Joyce and Jeannette all living there.

To sort out the bedrooms just for the weekend, Marjorie let Ida sleep in her bed, so we put a large mattress on the floor next to the bed, and put covers on that for Marjorie.

On a Sunday morning, we always had a roast dinner. We would have the kitchen range fire built up, poked it and when it was red hot under the oven, started to cook the roast dinner and pudding. After breakfast, Ida and our family went off to church. Being the organist, Harold had to wait back at church at the end of the service, and we went home ahead.

When we arrived home, my dad opened the door and said,

"The house is on fire!"

He was in a terrible state. I ran across the road to our friends' house because they had a telephone, to ring the fire brigade. The firemen arrived and worked very fast. They threw all the burning bedding through the window, and there were feathers everywhere!

It seems the fire had started in the bedroom where we had made the put-you-up bed. The firemen said some sparks from the kitchen range had shot up the chimney, and being an older house, the midfeather in the chimney had broken, and the sparks had landed on the mattress. Dad had seen the first signs of it, as smoke was coming from under the door to that room.

Dad had kept cages of budgerigars in the small room nearby. Sadly, smoke inhalation killed them all.

All our wedding presents were thrown out of the upstairs window either burnt or water damaged. It was a terrible scene. However, we were insured and the money we received for compensation provided us with a lump sum. This gave us the idea of putting a deposit on our own house.

Lynwood Gardens

After this episode, we decided it was time to buy our own house. Harold and I with our three girls moved to Lynwood Gardens, which was half way between my mum and dad's in Rawcliffe Road, and Harold's mum's at Orrell Park; so I was able to help both of them.

When we moved to this semi-detached house, it took all our savings, but we felt great, and loved it. Harold didn't sleep well for a couple of weeks, thinking of all that mortgage. He used to say,

> "Remind me not to read that statement!"

After paying back each month, with compound interest, we only owned one row of bricks. It was hard making ends meet for a few years, but eventually it started to ease up.

Televisions were creeping in for most families now. Joyce came home one day and said,

> "I am the only girl in our class without a television."

> "I am the only man in our office without a television,"

added Harold.
So I said,

> "I am the only mother in our road without a television!"

We did make jokes at times.

When the three girls were all growing up, I made most of their dresses. I would buy a length of material, and make all three the same pattern. I would always make them some new clothes before going on holiday. At the last minute I would be finishing off buttons and fasteners, with Harold saying,

"Come on, hurry up!"

He always threatened he would put the sewing machine in the boot of the car with the luggage! Even when we went for days out, I would always have 'another job' to finish first, so we did get used to him saying,

"Come on, come on! Chop, chop!"

As the organist at church, Harold did have to go earlier, to play the 'voluntary' as people were coming in. As always, I would have 'another job' to finish, and he would be saying,

"Come on, come on! You'll have me late."

One particular Sunday, we arose, had breakfast, and I was sorting the dinner out, preparing the vegetables. When I looked at the clock it said nearly eleven o'clock, and I thought it must be fast, because Harold had picked up the paper, and had started to read. Eventually, I said to him,

"What is the time? Is the clock fast?"

He calmly replied,

"No, it is not fast. I am not going to be shouting 'Come on!' any more."

I was shocked! We rushed out, and arrived at church. The church warden was standing at the gate saying,

"We can't start! We thought you were ill!"

Harold simply said,

"Blame my wife!"

I felt terrible! But guess what? We were never late again!

Dentist

Another incident comes to mind from that time. Our dentist had his practice on that main road up towards Aintree and I started with toothache. He was a very nice middle-aged dentist who we knew quite well. I had booked an appointment and was duly called in.
He had quite a modern set up and as you sat down he lowered the head rest of the seat so that your head went back, then the mirror was drawn across and the tube with water filtering through placed in your mouth whilst he did the fillings.

I sat down and he began with this procedure; the drill started then after a few moments it stopped and I thought he had found another tooth that needed filling. Nothing seemed to be happening except the water was still filtering into my mouth, so I tried to look up and then saw the dentist just staring into space. Next, I shook his arm and asked,

"Are you all right?"

No answer.

So I managed to take this tube put of my mouth, push the mirror back and scramble out of the seat. He still sat looking into space, so I ran through to reception to tell them. Fortunately, they knew that it was a mild form of epilepsy called a 'petit mal'; he had suffered one attack before, but never with a patient. His son, who was also a dentist, said that he would have to retire now.

It could only happen to me!

Hong Kong

Harold's brother, Syd, had been at sea for a number of years now, and had passed through to being a Master Marine. When he was on a trip to Hong Kong, he had a call from his company, the Alfred Hold Line, offering him a senior job on the wharf. They told him to send for his wife and any family, all costs covered – but of course he wasn't married! So they suggested he invite his mother (as she was a widow) to go out for nine months.

His mother, on hearing this news, nearly took fright! She had never been any further than the Isle of Man, and only with the family. She also suffered with a stomach ulcer, and had to be careful with her diet. However, Syd was so eager for her to have this holiday. He sent her money to buy some new clothes – she would be mixing with the ships' officers.

Harold's mother, Gladys Pierce

The liners they had then were cargo ships, with only a small area for officers' wives, when they were allowed to join the ship. Well, this journey was to take six weeks at sea! – And through the Bay of Biscay.

However, I went shopping with her and she said to me,

"If I don't make the journey there and back, you can have these clothes!"

She really was quite brave. She decided to go to the doctor and ask him about this sea journey. He gave her a prescription of tablets to take with her.

Then the day arrived for the departure. She was so fond and attached to our children; we all went down to the docks. The ship she was sailing on was the *'Cyclops'*, a Greek name. We were invited to have a light tea with her on board, and then went to her cabin, before leaving the ship. It was quite sad, for all of us, waving the *Cyclops* off, and wondering how she would cope.

Incidentally, this trip began a few days before Christmas, which made it harder to face then. So we went home, and carried on with life, then after a couple of weeks, we received a letter, which we opened in great haste. To our surprise she said the tablets the doctor had given her worked like a miracle! All on board had been invited to dinner on Christmas Day to the captain's table. Only four had been well enough to attend and yes! She was one of them!

She related how she was sliding from top to bottom in her bunk when going through the Bay of Biscay. She began to enjoy the days at sea. She was very well looked after.
Eventually she arrived at Hong Kong, and Syd gave her a wonderful time; she had servants to do all the work, and she adjusted to the amazingly different way of life and culture. Syd would take her out in a glass bottom boat in the lagoons, and she could choose any fish swimming she would like for her next meal! It all must have suited her digestion as she came back a few stones heavier!

Nine months seemed a long time, and then a letter arrived telling us when she was coming home again. We all went down to the docks to meet her. Then when she was home and settled in, she opened her large case, and it was like Aladdin's Cave. She brought lots of Chinese garments for the children, and Chinese toys. Her case had a wonderful smell of the Orient!

She loved going to Hong Kong so much, she made four journeys over the next few years, and each time was just as exciting. Syd never married; he became an Ex-Master Marine, and was very much attached to the Free Masons. He always had a major domo who looked after his house and welfare. Syd, in his time, travelled the world, but settled in Hong Kong for the rest of his life.

Buckingham Palace

At this period Harold used to play the organ for St Nathaniel's church, close to where we lived. Then the children joined the Brownies and Guides at St. John's church, also near home, and Marjorie became a Queen's Guide. She also decided to do the Duke of Edinburgh's Award Scheme. It was the beginning of a course introduced by the Duke of Edinburgh, involving teenagers working on different levels of achievement – starting with a bronze medal, then silver, and lastly gold. The silver award, which was quite tough to achieve, was presented at the Town Hall in Liverpool. Parents were invited to an afternoon tea, looked after by the flunkies in uniform, served with the town hall china. Then all moved to the court room, to be presented with the medal. All three of the girls achieved the silver medal.

Marjorie went on and completed the gold. When you reached gold, you were presented with the medal at Buckingham Palace. So we all went to Buckingham Palace to see the presentation of the Gold Medals. It was very special. First we had to attend meetings when we were informed of the protocol – what we could wear, no cameras, no stiletto heel shoes, and we were given large blue crosses to stick on our cars, as a recognition so we could drive into the grounds.

Sadly it rained heavily the day we went and the ceremony was held outside. All the ladies were wearing new outfits and hats which went floppy in the wet. Although it was a day to remember, the weather did mar the moment. We were taken into the

Royal Mews to see all the treasures in large glass cases, given to the Royal Family from their travels. We also went into the department where all the Royal Carriages were kept, and into the stables, where the horses were looked after. We all stayed in London for a couple of days, and enjoyed the sight seeing.

Mum and Dad

It was round about this stage in life when my mother was starting to deteriorate. Ida, who was now a Senior Tutor for midwifery, decided to come back to Liverpool from Sheffield. She applied for a tutor's post at Sefton General Hospital, and was able to buy a cosier house locally, to take mum and dad to live with her. As cars were more available for the working man, she had bought an Austin Mini, and also had her own telephone. (No more running down to the main road to make a phone call!)

So all was settled for a time, and she could take our parents out in the car. Then mother had to have the doctor out, and she was diagnosed with breast cancer, with about six months to live. We didn't let her go into hospital; Ida and I nursed her between us. Ida set up a trolley (being trained) and we coped between us. Dad at that point was still working, and the others in the family visited her during the day, and helped where they could. She didn't last the six months, and sadly died early 1961.

Dad was very lost now without her, and although he seemed fit and well, and still working in his early 70's, he too began to go down hill, and had to see the doctor. When he was sent for an x-ray, he was diagnosed with renal cancer. He had to have a major operation, and seemed to progress at first, but then relapsed. Again Ida and I decided to nurse him at home, and we did the same as for mum. He died just 15 months later than Mum.

Brenda, Marjorie and President Kennedy

My brother's family was reaching teenage years. They hadn't done badly at school, and were applying for jobs. Dorothy the eldest, now had a boyfriend; - I think she was working in a dentist's. The next down was Brenda – she would be about 18, and worked in an office at the ICI in Prescot. She also had a boyfriend, who had a motorbike. They decided to have a run out one evening – it was the same night that President Kennedy was shot and died. When the news about the President came through on the radio, I was just thinking,

> "How terrible",

when the phone rang. I picked up the receiver to hear my brother Reg telling me that his daughter Brenda and her boyfriend had both been killed on the road. They had been attempting to overtake an oil tanker when a car was coming the other way. Both car and bike swerved the same way, and crashed. The boy was an only son.

When Marjorie arrived home, she hadn't heard any of the awful news and she was all excited and couldn't wait to tell us that John had proposed to her and they were going to get engaged. What a night to choose!

We went to the funerals of Brenda and her boyfriend, both packed with young people. I mentioned earlier that Nell, Reg's wife, had had a nervous breakdown, and we hoped it wouldn't recur. Thankfully it didn't, but it did take some living with, and overcoming.

As I related earlier, Kenneth, Reg's elder son, was so bitter, he became an atheist. The vicar of the church who had officiated at Brenda's funeral service, called on the family repeatedly, and was concerned for them. He asked Kenneth to come to a meeting he had arranged, and he did go. The vicar talked and talked to Kenneth, so much that he joined that church, and all the activities, and later became a pastor himself! It was a revelation to us. The youngest son, Norman, was quite a comedian, (as they breed them in Liverpool!). When Kenneth came home between his training, Norman would say,

"Here's your prodigal arrived!"

Meanwhile in my sister Gladys's family, her two elder boys, Brian and Ian, decided to emigrate – Brian to South Africa, and Ian to Canada. Brian was married to a nurse, and they left England. In the sixties they lived in Johannesburg. They had a daughter, Lara, (who is married herself now). They were out there for years, but had divorced when Brian eventually decided to return to England. As Gladys was then living on her own, Brian moved in and has stayed with her, although he still visits his daughter from time to time in South Africa.

Now Ian and his wife Winnie stayed in Canada two years, but didn't settle to it, so returned. They had three children, who are all doing well.
Irene, Gladys's eldest daughter, a lovely girl, married Bill, who was a Master Marine Engineer, so was away a lot of the time. He is retired now, so back home permanently.
They have two children and also quite a few grandchildren have arrived since those days.

On the Edge

One of our excursions before we had our own car was a holiday in Wales. Harold had recently passed for his driver's licence and Ida let us borrow her car occasionally. This time Ida came with us as well, making six, so she hired a car and took Marjorie whilst Harold drove Ida's car with me and the other two girls. We wanted to explore more inland in Wales so we bought maps and duly set off. I think Ida was having a few problems with the hired car as she wasn't familiar with that make. However we made the journey to Llanfyllin and decided to have a ride around Lake Vyrnwy. We were particularly interested as this lake was flooded to make a reservoir and that is where Liverpool's water comes from.

On the map there was a road leading round the reservoir, however it turned out to be a very narrow path and about a third of the way up we began to panic as there was only enough room for one car, it was very steep with a sheer drop to the lake. We looked for somewhere to turn round to go back but with two cars it seemed impossible.

Then we saw a workman walking towards us and he said,

> "You shouldn't be here, this is not a public way, you will have to go back."

We said,

> "How?"

He told us that there was a little cut-out up the side of the hill, further along and we would have to reverse up it and turn round. When we reached it we stopped the cars and Harold said,

> "I will go first, drive past it and reverse up a bit and round."

Opposite this little rough slope was the path, just one car's width, and a bit of a fence before the drop. So with bated breath, Harold slowly reversed back up this cut out incline and brought the car round with me and the girls still in it, leaving it at the edge. He then went to see to Ida. She took one look and said,

> "I can't do it"

Then Harold said,

"You will have to do it. I can't chance a hired car that is not in my name."

And he made her get into the car and stood in front of her, next to the drop while she carefully reversed her car back up the slope. If she had slipped, he would have been knocked into the lake ahead of her. It was so frightening!

However, she did make it and we drove back off the track to the road. We stopped and Ida got out of the car and fainted. She was shaking so much, but after a hot drink felt better.

But that night in bed, I must have had travel sickness, because as I closed my eyes, the fields and posts were flying past me and I had to mentally grab a post and cling on to stop the movement in my mind.

A Testing Time

In the 1930's to the 1960's, most people smoked cigarettes, and some of the older men smoked cigars or pipes. It was the custom to go to the cinema, sit down, and light up a cigarette. We had no idea how damaging to the health this habit was, and the cinemas would be thick with smoke. When we went to a dance, the cigarettes were handed round. In fact you felt a bit naïve if you didn't smoke. At Christmas time, Harold would receive wooden boxes full of cigarettes as presents from clients and other firms they dealt with. He used to call the week before Christmas 'Bribery and Corruption Week'! However, these cigarettes did not last all year, and they did cost money.

Now the motor car was beginning to come within the reach of working people, Harold decided he would like to have one. His mother (who was now receiving a generous allowance from Syd in Hong Kong) said she would let us have some money towards it, as she probably would have outings at times, and she was a really good mother-in-law, and idolised the grandchildren. Harold came home from work the very next day and said,

> "I have stopped smoking because I am buying a car, and I don't want to have to count how many cigarettes I can buy as well as keep the car on the road."

So we all went to choose our new car. It was a Vauxhall Viva.

Later the news and the advertisements started informing people about the ill effects of smoking. It was realized how lungs were being damaged. So then I decided to give it up myself. Oh, but it was habit-forming, and took much determination to pack up. I thought to myself,

> "If I can get through Christmas time without a cigarette, I will be free."

And I did!

When we bought our first car it was of great importance. Many families now had one and we felt we were moving up in the world. Harold had been driving vehicles during the war, in the desert, but this was something new. He had a refresher course and took a test for his driving licence. It seemed so wonderful not to be waiting for public transport, but then, as with all things, you do get familiar.

Ida and Harold had both passed their tests first time. Then Marjorie turned 17 and she wanted to learn to drive and also passed first time. The time came when I was being encouraged to learn. I was a bit reluctant at first so we bought some new L-plates and began. Harold gave me the first lessons in quiet areas to start off with. Then I went to a school of motoring for some tuition before my test. I always thought that I would be the first to fail, so when I got the date of the test, I decided that I would not tell anyone. I did not want them all wondering how I was doing and then to have to go home and say that I had failed!

So the morning came; Harold went off to work and the children to school. We had an hour's practice first but everything went wrong. The instructor told me that I was just wasting his time; he and I had never got on well and I nearly told him to take me home.

However, the time arrived and I drove to the test centre. We had to wait for our names to be called, I had been nervous before but now the adrenalin began to flow. My name was called out and two men, not one, came over to me. I was informed that the second chap was testing the tester! He would sit in the back and that he was nothing to do with me. I decided that I had no chance since the examiner would really be on his metal.

However, we all got into the car and I had to start up. When I came to do the reverse up a side road, the second fellow lay down on the back seat to make sure that he wasn't interfering with my view. At the end I parked the car and waited for the test questions; I was quite dithery. Then I waited for the final results. When I saw him bring out that pink slip which meant I had passed, I really could not believe it!

I took it home and put it up on the shelf over the fireplace and waited.

Jeannette was the first home and when I told her, she went into the next room and came out with a paper parcel, saying

"This is the very present for you."

Ever the practical joker, she had put this gadget inside the paper bag which was a pin with an elastic band wound tightly round it. When she put it in my hand, the thing sprang to life and jumped about inside the bag. It made me jump and I was already shaking, I dropped it quickly!

Then later, when Harold came home, I stayed in the kitchen, making the tea, waiting for him to notice the pink slip. He was reading the paper but suddenly noticed and said,

"You so and so, you never even told us!"

I had passed first time!

Scotland for the Brave

When the children were quite young, most families were only able to travel on holiday to places by train or bus and because wages were moderate, we could only afford to go to fairly local places. It was still exciting to pack up the baby's pram (which had a well under the seating) with the children's clothes and take the local train into Liverpool and then get another steam train from Lime Street Station to various parts of Wales. There were nearly always big queues waiting for the next train.

When we bought our first new car, it was now a chance to explore the places we only knew by name such as Scotland, Cornwall, Northumberland, and to really get round the Lake District. So we bought maps to study and follow the chosen route.

We decided on and booked a two week holiday in Scotland at a place called Arrochar on the shores of Loch Long. We had two cars, as the whole family was going, including Ida and Harold's mother, Gladys. Harold called us his 'Harem'.

The scenery was breathtaking and we had booked Bed and Breakfast at a large bungalow with a long gravel path leading down to the edge of the loch. When we went out each day we had to travel along the side of the loch for many miles, there was only one way in and out. We always passed a place called 'Rest and Be Thankful' where there stood a Scotsman among the fields playing tunes on the bagpipes. The road went up and then down really steeply several times and the children christened it the 'Ooh! Mee Tummy' road.

Breakfasts were always very jolly with such a gang of us. As the week passed we invented a tongue twister and each day we kept adding a bit more. It ended up as,

> "Should a sleepy Sassenach suck a second succulent Scottish sausage successfully?"

I heard someone say this on the radio fairly recently, so it must have spread out into the world! But just for the record, we invented it!

The weather had been fine and sunny while driving up to Scotland but the next day it started to rain, and it rained and rained and rained.

One day we drove to Oban, ran into a café and had a snack, then drove all the way back to the bungalow. The next day we tried the Trossachs, drove into the car park, but the mist was so bad that we didn't stop. We drove straight out again and back to Arrochar.
Other days we pulled into lay-bys and played games in the car, it was so wet. With all the rain the water at Loch Long had reached a couple of feet from the door of the bungalow.

One of the most memorable days was our visit to the Highland Games in Dunoon. It was a new experience for us seeing events such as the highland dancing, the pipe band competition and tossing the caber. In the evening there was a huge parade through the narrow streets with the massed pipe bands all playing different tunes as they came past. Our ears rang with the noise all night afterwards.

After 8 days we had had enough of the continual rain, and decided to go home. We drove over to the East coast to travel down the coast line, and at Seahouses the sun came out! We decided to stay the night. We visited Lindisfarne, Holy Island, and the weather was beautiful. Over the next week we worked our way back and enjoyed the experience.

In later years we did have some beautiful holidays in different parts of Scotland.

Even quite recently, Joyce and I took a week's holiday in Dumfries and Galloway. We visited friends in Auchencairn and decided to go and watch the tattoo in Kirkcudbright one evening. We got there early and found a good place to stand. It was all very enjoyable with a whole variety of entertainments including dog trials, Scottish dancing and different sorts of bands. As the evening started to darken they suddenly lit up a window near the top of a ruined castle, near the harbour, and a lone piper in full highland dress appeared playing beautiful traditional melodies. It was very touching, it seemed like another world.

Finally, as the evening drew to a close, the whole company and all the visitors formed a procession with flaming torches and we paraded right through the village. It was spectacular. There was a bucket of water at the end for each one to douse the flames and then we had to get back to our guest house, at midnight, in the pitch dark.

Back to Work

All the embroidery business began to diminish. The shipping in Liverpool had slowed down, all the main trading went down to Southampton, and the docks closed. As my children were getting a bit older, I decided to apply for a new job, with no more jerseys to sew.

I did work in sales at one of the big stores for a couple of years. I started on part time, and Harold's mother would baby sit and meet Joyce and Jeannette from school, (Marjorie was older then). In the few years I worked at T.J.Hughes, I met a lovely group of friends.

Rose was my first – we started going to night school classes together. Her husband Arthur was also very sociable, so we became a foursome, and went away together over the next forty years. There were other friends from work we fell in with, Rose and I, and formed a group. There was Manny, and her husband Roger, Maisie and John, (whose wartime escapade I have mentioned), Kathy and her husband, Rose and Arthur, and then Harold and I.

We had days out together, and occasional arrangements to meet at the various houses, for a meal – no dining at restaurants then! We all had children growing up, so would chat about them. We had some wonderful times in that group, but only Rose and Arthur went away on holiday with Harold and me.

As aeroplane flights and holidays abroad were becoming popular, we thought we would chance going to Austria for two weeks – our first great adventure! Rose was terrified, so went to the doctor's, and he gave her some pills to calm her down. However, she did relax, and travelled with us alright. It was a wonderful experience flying over the clouds, and we had a great fortnight's holiday. Even now, I still think it was special although we did many flights later.

We stayed very close friends to the end. Harold died first, then years later, Arthur had a stroke, and a couple of years later, Rose died. Where did all those years disappear to?

Between all those years, I moved to another job. I saw an advert, asking for a clerk in Liverpool's Northern Hospital, so sent off for an application form. Even in my younger days I had always wanted an office job. I then had an interview and was accepted. So I started, and I was so delighted! It was an interesting and more challenging job and I enjoyed all the years I was there.

When I decided to go back to work, education had advanced, and girls as well as boys had opportunities to pass exams for the grammar schools. If they were clever then they could choose a career rather than take any job that came along. One of these careers was as a medical secretary for which they learnt shorthand, typing and medical terminology. When I started work in the Northern Hospital, I was in the same office as the medical secretaries but my job was as a clerk on various clinics. I had to collect the case notes and check that all requested reports such as blood tests and X-rays were all complete in the files ready for the doctors to see in the clinic.

In those days most of the case notes were filed on shelves in the basement of the hospital. It was like going through a maze in a cavern, with no windows. A set of switches for the lights was just on the entrance wall.

One day when I had gone well into the area and was collecting case notes for a particular clinic, the lights suddenly all went out and I was left in the pitch dark. One of the other clerks must have popped in for a file and as she left had switched the lights off, not realising that there was someone else there. I was lost and had to walk down the aisles between the shelves with my arms stretched out, touching each side. It was terrifying and it was also known that rats occasionally appeared in the basement! I kept walking along the passages until eventually I could see a chink of light from a grid in the wall. Later on the system was changed after a young girl had the same experience and went hysterical.

The office I worked in was divided into two sections; the new younger staff being in the other part. In the early days when working in a hospital no-one was allowed to run down corridors and you had to pay great respect to the senior staff such as tutors and doctors, hold doors open and so on. There was also a rule that there should always be one of the secretaries in the office in case of emergency and they were needed for dictation by the medical staff. However, the new age has a different attitude to discipline.

One afternoon when all seemed quiet, I was the only one around, for the young medical secretaries had all gone to lunch together. When one of the senior consultants walked in, he said to me,

> "I want an urgent letter taken down and sent off."

I replied,

> "I don't do shorthand, I am not a medical secretary but I can fix a tape for you."

He asked,

> "Where are they all?"

> "I think they have gone to lunch".

Well, he stalked up and down that room with his hands behind his back and said angrily,

> "Gone are the days of respect. If you complain they tell you to 'drop dead' and they even let the doors shut in your face!"

He then sat down and used the tape to dictate his letter, so I crept out!!!

In the 70's, it was a new idea to amalgamate all the General Hospitals in Liverpool into one huge hospital, the Royal Liverpool. The staff who worked in the hospitals that were closing down had to transfer all the case notes over to the Royal, and inform all the patients. Each hospital specialised in different illnesses, so it was a real task, tracing all the case notes for each clinic, - they were all stored in basements, libraries, on wards, sometimes in a different hospital if the patient had attended there, and even in doctors' cars! They all had to go through microfiche, and the doctors would not see the patient until the case notes were in his file.

The appointments for patients attending hospital went into thousands per hospital. The whole project was all time-and-motion studied, and the six designated hospitals were to amalgamate within two years. Where we had previously been dealing with about a dozen specialists, this new hospital was dealing with nearly a hundred. The postman came with mail by the sack load. It all had to be put into the various doctors' baskets, in brackets on a huge wall. It was fine if the G.P. had addressed the letter to a specific consultant, but if it was only the medical department that was quoted, we had a quandary as to which basket to put it in. Some of the consultants only dealt with very special cases, and we were in trouble if we put a letter in the wrong basket!

The new hospital had three dining rooms; one even had an 'à la carte' menu. The lifts were all electrically operated, there were nearly thirty x-ray cubicles with a desk which registered which one was empty, and even an on-site bank. With all the equipment for all the various therapies and techniques, I used to say,

"No-one could die here!"

With everything starting to be computerised, it was certainly a great time for change and advancement, and we had to attend several courses in Rodney Street, including using computers, to prepare for all the new ways of working.

Stopping the Traffic

A few years afterwards, I was meeting up with my group of friends from T J Hughes. We had made arrangements to meet at Maisie and John's house, near Maghull. Then my daughter Marjorie rang and invited us over for a birthday celebration. She lived in Greasby on the Wirral. It being a Sunday, we also had Ida and my Auntie Amy, who was then about 83, with us.

Now, after dinner I said that I would like to call on Maisie to explain that I couldn't go this time, before going on to Marjorie's. I decided to go in Harold's car with Auntie Amy and the rest of the family would go in Ida's car.

Going to Marjorie's entailed travelling through the (then 'new') underground road tunnel from Liverpool to the Wirral. So I set off with Auntie Amy to Maghull and I did notice that the petrol was low but after chatting to Maisie and then to Auntie Amy who was asking all about these friends, I found myself entering the tunnel.

I paid the toll and started on my way through. It travels down hill gradually for a while, then starts to climb up again. As we reached this part the car started to judder and I suddenly remembered the petrol; cars did not give reminders in those days when petrol was needed.

We stopped! The rules of the tunnel were very strict; **NO-ONE MUST GET OUT OF THEIR CAR.** There was a large penalty if they did. I knew that this car had an extra petrol tank and that there was a switch in the boot but I had never used it before.

I was on the spot; I just had to sit while I watched the cars behind me piling up in a huge queue, right back to the entrance. After what seemed an age, a police car came up at the side and asked me what the matter was. I had to tell them that I had no petrol.

I did explain that I could open the boot and turn on the extra tank. He reminded me of the penalty of stepping out of the car, then proceeded to connect a strong wire to the front of my car from his. He pulled me over to the slow lane and drove out. The wire was like elastic and I nearly ran into the back of him; I had to keep putting my foot on the brake.

Eventually we came to the exit and he pulled me over to the left, over some building rubble as lots of work was still being done. He got out and came round to me saying'

"Now, prove to me you have some petrol."

Well, I had never had to open the boot and use this thing in the back, but there were instructions on how to do it that I had to read, with a big policeman standing over me. I did what it said, but when I tried to start the car up, it wouldn't start as it was on an upward angle on this rubble.

Anyway, he said that he would try for me; he could only just fit in, but did get it started which was a great relief to me. He then said that we would have to go up to the office to pay the penalty for stopping, but seeing as I did have some petrol, he would halve it.

So we went to the office and the first thing they asked me for was the car registration number. I went cold. I could only remember the first couple of letters as I always considered that it was Harold's car. I was worried that they would think it was a stolen car and as I was stuttering an explanation, the policeman opened his hand and on his palm, he had written the number down in ball point pen! The outcome was that I had to pay £6.50, half price.

Now all this took another hour and when I got back in the car, I had to turn it round over all that rubble and proceed to

Marjorie's in Greasby. When we arrived the family all came out, -

"Where have you been? We thought you must have been in an accident."

When I explained all, Marjorie took out her diary and printed,

"MOTHER RAN OUT OF PETROL IN THE TUNNEL"

Cornwall - Launceston

We thought it would be a good idea to have a holiday near Cornwall for two weeks as we were starting to feel a bit more affluent by now. We planned a route and I looked through all the brochures and found a guest house that seemed suitable for all the family and Ida who was joining us. It was a large guest house in Launceston, adjoining Bodmin Moor. So we booked it a couple of months earlier and looked forward to going. It was about 350 miles travelling and we decided to spend one night at Bath on the way down and the same when travelling back.

The day dawned and we all set off. It was warm, sunny weather and we had a nice stay at Bath. We didn't leave Bath very early as we had a good look round first. We then set off for Bodmin and by the time we arrived it was about 7pm. It was a beautiful area and this guest house was in a lovely setting with a tree lined path to drive through. The owners came out to greet us. We said that we would drop the luggage off and go for a meal as we had only had a picnic lunch, and so we went in.

They were a young married couple and only new to having holiday guests. They showed us a couple of rooms upstairs which seemed quite nice and then showed us the room for two of the children, downstairs.

Now, this room was only a wooden annexe. It was just big enough for a camp bed each side and a small dressing table but as we walked into this annexe, it smelt musty and damp; it reminded me of the air raid shelter during the war. When I remarked on it, the young lady said that she would put a heater in to warm the room whilst we went for our meal.

We finished our meal and had a little walk round Launceston before bed. We happily went back to this guest house; it would be near 10pm by now. However, as we walked into the annexe room with the heater in it, it smelt terrible like warmed up damp, stale flock mattresses. I said to Harold,

"We can't let the children sleep in here, especially Joyce after her chest problems."

So Harold said,

"Well, let them have our room and we will sleep here."

That seemed OK. We saw the children to bed in the upstairs rooms with Ida and we proceeded to get undressed and into bed. Now, these beds were only camp beds with flock mattresses and flock pillows and still smelt all musty and damp. I got into the far side one and I could feel the damp rising. Remember we were on Bodmin Moor and it was freezing, also the smell was making me feel sick. I complained so much that Harold suggested that we change beds.

"You have this one,"

he said. So we swapped, but that was worse. This wooden shack leant onto the wall of the house where the toilet was and I could hear other folks going into the toilet and pulling the chain. I was in a pink, silk nightdress and, by now, shivering.

I lost my temper, jumped out of bed, stormed to the door, opened it and shouted,

> "Is there anyone about, I am not suffering this room any more."

A great big Alsatian dog came bounding down the hall towards me. I slammed the door shut and eventually the man came down to ask what the matter was. I asked him,

> "Would you sleep in either of these beds? Smell them. Just swap your beds for these."

He agreed to fix us up in a bed in the living room where there was a settee which folded out to make a double bed. He put clean white cotton sheets on but they were freezing cold too. Now in this room was a serving hatch and on the other side was this huge Alsatian dog which we could hear mooching round. We did get into this bed but by now I was too cold and shivering; the thought that the dog might come through the hatch terrified me. I slept for just a couple of hours but when it came light I got up and dressed and went for a walk. I knew they would need the room for breakfast soon, anyway.

When I got back, I said to Harold,

> "We are not staying on here; I'm going, even though we have booked for two weeks."

Then his wife came to me, she was sobbing and saying,

> "Please don't go. I will explain what has happened. A car drew up at the guest house yesterday with a couple from London and they asked if there were any vacancies."

So, what did they do? They had given them our room which we had booked months before. Then they had hastily collected the camp beds from an outside shed and made them up for us.

My reply was,

> "Do you think that because we come from Liverpool that's what my children are used to? We had better beds in our air raid shelter during the war. Let me tell you, my children have modern, spring mattresses on a proper single bed each. So, I am packing up and going."

She was still very upset and said that her husband had gone straight into town to buy new mattresses, and that she wouldn't charge us for bed and breakfast for today.
I replied that she should have done that first.

So, we packed up the car and moved on. It did leave us adrift because we now had to find somewhere else to stay. I think we did bed and breakfast at various places on the way back to Bath. After that it was straight home.

So much for these 'posh' places!

Marjorie

During this time, Marjorie was taking her 'A' Levels, and planning to apply for college for a teaching career. Half-way through her A level year, she changed her mind. She had met a boy friend, so perhaps did not want to move away. After much deliberation, she went into town, and signed on to start a nursing career at the Royal Liverpool Hospital. Her dad said to her,

> "Don't come back crying when you have to empty bed pans on Christmas Day!"

She did make a successful career of it and went on to be a health visitor. Later, she took a B.A. degree with the Open University.

She and John did get married, and she carried on working for about six years, until she started with her first baby.

She had reached five months of pregnancy when things started to go wrong, and sadly had a miscarriage – it was a little boy. It took her time to recover, but she did. They were living on The Wirral, in Greasby at this point. She went back to work until she started with her next baby – thankfully a healthy lovely little girl named Sarah. Two and a half years later, they had another little girl, Ruth, and then Judith a few years later again. Three lovely daughters, like me!

While living on the Wirral, Marjorie and John became members of their local church. John trained as a lay reader. Marjorie at that time was a health visitor, working part time as she had Sarah as a young child. I usually went over to their house each Thursday to baby-sit and help out and Harold would come over at tea time straight from work. We would go home late evening.

They were quite friendly with the neighbours. A few doors up lived Marion and her husband. They had come to live there after her only daughter married and emigrated to Canada. They both went out to work as they now had this mortgage to pay. Her daughter had a little girl, Sharon, who was now 5½ years old. Marion had never seen this little girl, because folk didn't have that much extra money for travel abroad then, but they had photographs of her.

One evening, near to Christmas, Marion called at Marjorie's house in a very distressed state. She had received a phone call from Canada telling her that her daughter and son-in-law had been killed in a road accident and that Sharon was being cared for, temporarily. The authorities then decided that she would have to be sent to her grandparents in England.

Marion was so shocked that she was unable to think properly. So Marjorie gave it some thought and as Marion could not give up her job because of the mortgage, she offered to mind the little girl on her days off, to help. So, when I went over on a Thursday, I cared for her along with Sarah.

On my first visit with them both, I played with them until Sarah, only 10 months old, needed a sleep after her dinner. Then I said to Sharon,

>"Would you like to play a game?"

thinking she would like Snakes and Ladders or Dominoes, when she said,

>"I can play chess!"

I replied,

>"Well, I can't play chess".

So we looked in the games cupboard and there was Monopoly. She said,

>"I can play that. Can I be banker?"

I was amazed but agreed and we started playing. After a while Sarah woke up and she was crying upstairs. I said that I must go and get her, but Sharon said,

>"No, don't go. Leave her to cry like I had to."

>"No, I will bring Sarah down"

I think she thought that I was spoiling the game. When I went upstairs I could hear Marjorie's little black and white dog howling. She had grabbed the dog by its tail and was twisting it round and round really tightly. I think the poor child was so traumatized by what had happened to her.

E.A.Pierce June 2008

By now it was 4pm and the schools were out. The two girls from next door came in to play. John had made a lovely wooden slide with steps up one side, a platform on the top and a slide down the other side. Now, as Sharon came sliding down, she saw a Christmas card on the settee with Christ and the shepherds. She picked it up and said to me,

"Why did he let my mummy and daddy get killed?"

I honestly could not explain to a little girl of 5½ years. Marion and John did have a great deal of stress and worry with her for quite a number of years. I guess she has adjusted and is living a normal life today; poor child!

Joyce

My second daughter, Joyce, had reached the age to sit for the scholarship, and she passed, and followed Marjorie to Holly Lodge. She excelled in maths. She had a bit of a set back when she started having trouble with her chest again. I was quite worried and took her back to the hospital to see Mr. Bickford. He remembered her, and was lovely with her. He sent her for x-rays, and we had to go back for an appointment ten days later. The result was,

"Nothing to do with bronchiectasis," he said.

"In fact the lung she was operated on has started to grow. It's her sinuses causing this problem."

She did have to have another operation to stop the sinuses filling up. For all the times she was away from school, she still did well.

Marjorie and Joyce had started to attend St. Matthew's Church in Bootle. A church trip was arranged to a holiday place on the

Wirral, for the youth group and confirmation class, and Joyce wanted to go. I think she was about 14½ years old. On this holiday she met a boy named James. He was a year older, and was at Merchant Taylor's Grammar School. At first I thought she was too young, but he was a very nice, polite boy, and became part of our family. They would do homework together.

Jim, as he became known later, came from a large family: an elder brother John, who was married, an elder sister Dorothy, also married, another older sister, Barbara, who had started nursing training, then two younger brothers, Kenneth and David. During Jim's time at Merchant Taylor's, his father had a fatal aneurism. He had been a dairyman, and owned a shop. When he died, Jim's mother moved out of the shop to a smaller house with Jim and his two younger brothers, along with Barbara when she was off duty.

What they came to realise, was that his mother had moved to make life easier for Barbara and the boys, because she had been diagnosed with breast cancer, and only had a short time to live.

Jim's father had been a Free Mason, so when the time came, after their mother died, the Masons arranged for Kenneth to go to a naval training college, and for David to go to Scarisbrick boarding school. This meant that Jim was more or less alone when Barbara was working. He had an aunt who kept in touch, and then he had our house, and Joyce to visit.

He was reaching his 'A' Levels, and thinking of university. He decided on studying for a London University degree, at Rugby College. The time came for his departure. He found it a bit hard and strange at first, but settled down and worked hard. We encouraged him and visited with Joyce, and were delighted when the day came for his degree ceremony.

He attained an honours degree in Mathematics and Science and then went into teaching. He was a deputy headmaster at a large comprehensive school for many years and later gained an M.Sc. in Education.

Joyce was one academic year behind Jim, so when she was doing her 'A' Levels, and choosing which university to apply to, she decided to go to Leicester to take Maths and Physics. In fact Leicester wasn't too far away from Rugby, so they did have times they managed to meet up.

Where we lived in Lynwood Gardens, we had three bedrooms, two large and one smaller. Growing up, Marjorie had the smaller one to herself, while Joyce and Jeannette shared the larger one with a single bed each. When Marjorie moved on to nursing, and had to move into the hospital, Jeannette moved from sharing with Joyce, into Marjorie's room. We redecorated and refurnished it for her. Before long, it was time for Joyce to move on to Leicester, so Jeannette (4½ years younger) was at home now, on her own with us. We visited Joyce in Leicester from time to time, and then the time eventually came for her degree ceremony at the De Montford Hall. She attained a first class honours degree.

Joyce also went into teaching after starting work with computers, and eventually became head of mathematics at a successful sixth form college. She also gained an M.Sc. in mathematics in later years after studying part-time with the Open University.

Jeannette

Jeannette also passed the scholarship, and followed on to Holly Lodge. She was very good at languages. Harold and I attended all the parents' evenings and speech nights, and the teachers would say,

"You must encourage your children to move on, and take responsibility, and not tie them to your apron strings."

Times were definitely changing; my age group growing up didn't move far from the neighbourhood.

So now, at 14, Jeannette had progressed really well with French, and the school was arranging French exchanges. All was set for her to have three weeks with a French family at Metz. We had to take her to London, and see the group off on the train to France.

After the three weeks, she came back with the French girl, Marie-Anne, to stay at our house for another three weeks. It was quite an experience! Most of our family had learned a bit of French at school, but not me. I would try talking to her, slowly and loudly. Jeannette would say,

"Mum, she's not deaf, and she doesn't want to learn broken English!"

We did have great fun. Many times we would be laughing, but Marie-Anne, with her limited English, did not grasp the joke. She said to Jeannette,

"I do not comprehend your mum, and when you are all together you laugh, and I don't know when to laugh!"

So Jeannette cut out a piece of white cardboard, and wrote,

"LAUGH NOW",

on it! So when we were all together, and any funny tales were being told, Jeannette would hold this card up, to include her in the merriment, and she would go into hysterics – in fact we all did! When Jeannette could find enough breath, she would try to translate the story to Marie-Anne, but many times the response was funnier than the original joke!

E.A.Pierce June 2008

One thing we learnt about France was that the evening meal takes all evening. Jeannette described how the mother would cook each item and serve it as a separate course, with time between each course as the next item was prepared. So the whole evening is spent round the table. Here in England, we have tea (evening meal) and quite often go out after.

At first Marie-Anne was so slow eating, we kept saying,

"Hurry up, we are going out!"

Well, by the end of the third week with us, she was gobbling up her tea, saying,

"We go where?"

Arnside

My first introduction to Arnside was in 1965. I had decided to go back to work after having the children with a long period at home. I started at T.J.Hughes, a large department store, in the stationery department. The next year I was moved to the shoe department where I met Rose, and as I've said, we immediately became close friends. Her husband, Arthur, and my husband, Harold also became friends, both being businessmen. From that moment on Rose and I enjoyed many activities together like night school classes and holidays as a foursome.

One summer, Arthur's mother was quite ill and when she was recovering, she was sent to Parkside in Arnside, part of the Grey Court Fellowship, to recuperate. Rose and Arthur went up to visit his mother and found out that it was not only a convalescent home but also a holiday guest house for families, with a Christian ethos.

Parkside, Arnside

Arnside is just past Morecambe at the south of the Lake District. So we decided to try it as we both had families then. The house is situated in lovely gardens with a bowling green and a putting green. It has beautiful views over the Kent Estuary. There were plenty of bedrooms and a large lounge/ballroom.

Each week there were activities, coach trips and walks organised by the host and hostess for the week. There were competitions for bowls and putting, games of whist and dominoes, fancy dress competitions and quizzes. In the evenings we danced and the guests would all join in to make the entertainment. We had never enjoyed ourselves so much. We never stopped laughing all week; we made friends with lots of lovely people and didn't want to go home at the end of the holiday. We were hooked!

We went each year for several years with more family, friends, neighbours and always had a really good time.

About ten years ago my daughter, Joyce, suggested that she and I have a holiday together as, by this time, Rose and Arthur and Harold had all passed away and I was on my own. She had an extra week's holiday that summer so she knew that her husband would not mind me taking up the time. She said that we could go anywhere I liked. It didn't take me long to think of Arnside. She was amazed as she had expected me to choose an exotic place abroad, somewhere like Greece or Portugal that I hadn't seen.

So ever since then we have had a week at Parkside each summer and thoroughly enjoyed it. We come back feeling much fitter for all the fresh air and exercise. It is not quite the same now as nearly everyone has a car and does their own thing during the day and there are mainly retired people rather than families, but we still have a good time with plenty of physical activities and usually a trip and a walk around the Lake District, which I love.

The Family Scattering

After a year at Leicester University, Joyce and Jim decided to get engaged. They came home for the summer and both took holiday jobs at T.J. Hughes, where I was working. They planned an engagement party and told everyone, including Harold's mum.

However, his mum rang Harold one evening saying that she felt poorly. Harold went to see her and they both thought she had eaten something that disagreed with her as she had bad indigestion. Sadly he had a phone call the next day from her neighbour to say that she had passed away in the night. Syd came home for the funeral and it was decided to continue with the engagement party a few weeks later. Gladys Pierce was sadly missed by all the family.

Joyce and James were engaged for two years, and their wedding day was arranged for shortly after Joyce's graduation. Harold had been helping them to find and buy a suitable house. Jim at this time was about to start teaching at Hyde, Cheshire, so they settled there and have lived in the Greater Manchester area ever since.

When it came to career choices, Jeannette decided to train as a teacher, so went to Alsager College, near Crewe, studying French and English Literature as well as Education for teacher training. Whilst there, a 3 month course was arranged, at the Institute Britannique in Paris, which had affiliation to the University of Paris. Whilst she was there, Harold and I had a holiday in Paris. It seemed funny, our youngest showing us round Paris, and waving us off at the airport when it came to leaving again!

Jeannette met her boyfriend, Karl, at College. Karl's mother was an Austrian. She had married one of the British soldiers after the war, and moved here. Jeannette and Karl got engaged, and the wedding was arranged. They needed to find a house around Blackburn, as Karl had a post in Rishton, and Jeannette was starting to teach French at a school in Darwen, both in the Blackburn area. Eventually a house was found, on a very steep hill in Blackburn. I said she could take her bedroom furniture for a second room.

Harold was now a manager for his firm and had access to borrowing the large vans. So the day was arranged to pick up the van and collect the furniture to take up to Jeannette's new house. At that time I was working at the hospital, so when I went home that afternoon, and as I knew all her belongings were going, went upstairs to see the state of things. My goodness! Harold had not only taken the furniture, but the curtains and carpet also! I walked into a completely empty room! I could have cried – the last one in the nest had gone! But instead of feeling sorry for myself, I said,

"This is life, and they are all responsible people now."

Then I went and made the tea for Harold and me.

The Next Generation

When Marjorie and John had been married for about six years they announced that they were expecting a baby. This was to be our first grandchild and we were all thrilled. Everything seemed to be going well until Easter Sunday morning. Harold and I were about to set out for church when Marjorie rang saying that she was having pains and had rung for the doctor; she was about 5 months pregnant. I decided that I would go over to her immediately and after a little thought Harold decided to ring the vicar, to say that he would not be available to play the organ that morning, and come with me.

We set off and by the time we arrived at their house on the Wirral, the ambulance was at their door, just closing up the back. When I jumped out of our car and ran to the ambulance, the driver asked me,

"Who are you?"

"Marjorie's mother"

So he opened the back again and let me travel with her. John, her husband had to go in his car as they were taking her to Parkgate Hospital, quite a journey, and it being a very rural area there would be no other transport to get home again. Half way there Marjorie began to haemorrhage. The ambulance had to stop and the man tipped her bed so that her feet were up. The driver then put on the siren and went as fast as possible to the hospital.

As a mother you try to protect your children from stresses and traumas to the best of your ability, but there comes a time when they have to face all these things themselves. So whilst we sped along, I talked to her and tried to ease some of the pain. As we arrived at the hospital, she was taken straight in and put on a drip, but sadly they could not save the baby. It was a fully formed little boy and lovely. The whole family was devastated.

It took Marjorie a long time to recover from the ordeal, both physically and emotionally, but eventually she became pregnant again and now has her three lovely girls who are grown up with children themselves.

Joyce and Jeannette both married as they finished their qualifications and, after a few years, they decided to start their families too. Joyce's pregnancies seemed straightforward which was a great relief considering all the times in hospital and operations when she was young.

When the girls had their babies I usually arranged to go and stay with them for a week after they came out of hospital. When

Jeannette was expecting her first child, Christine, she and Karl were living in Blackburn. The birth was fine so the day she was being discharged it was agreed that Harold and I would collect them from the nursing home, in Whalley and take them home as Karl would be teaching at his school in Rishton, and they didn't have a car at the time. Both Whalley and Rishton are a good way out from Blackburn.

Now when Harold was working he had full use of the car and I only borrowed it occasionally, if I needed to. All the long journeys, he would drive. Now sometimes, usually when under stress, Harold suffered bouts of sickness; the doctor called it 'Stomach Migraine'. On the Monday morning when we were due to pick up Jeannette, Harold woke up with one of his migraines and feeling terrible. We were expected at the hospital about 11am and en route we were to pick up a suitcase with all the baby clothes from Jeannette's house in Blackburn. I was in a bit of a dilemma. I couldn't leave Harold on his own in Liverpool and I wasn't used to driving the car such a long distance. I decided that Harold would have to lie on the back seat with a bucket in case he was sick and off we went. The traffic on a Monday morning was horrendous but I carried on, having to ask Harold the way. We arrived at Jeannette's house on Oozehead Lane in Blackburn but, guess what!! I could see the case to be picked up through the window but I had forgotten the key!

What now?

Harold, in the middle of being ill, suggested I go to the school in Rishton where Karl was a teacher and get his key. I had intended to put Harold in bed when we arrived at Jeannette's but first of all we couldn't get in and secondly I needed him to direct me to Karl's school. I looked at the map which did help and then eventually arrived at the school. We asked where we could find Karl and when he saw us he went pale and nearly fainted as he thought immediately that something had gone wrong with Jeannette or the baby. We reassured him, collected his key and I drove back to Blackburn. I opened the door, sorted the bed out for Harold, collected the suitcase of baby clothes and now had to find my way to the hospital in Whalley on my own!

I made it. I met Jeannette sitting there looking pale saying,

"Mum, you have been a long time. Did you bring any biscuits or chocolates for the nurses?"

The nurse dressed the baby and told me that Jeannette was a bit anaemic and feeling a bit dizzy, she needed to rest. Then I had to go to the village in the car and find a shop to buy these presents. All that done, we get mother and baby into the car. We had a navy blue carry cot and little baby Christine had been lying in a light perspex cot in the hospital so she cried and cried and never stopped all the way back to Blackburn. It was a relief that Jeannette knew the way.

We arrived home but Jeannette was still not feeling good, the baby never quietened down. I had to prepare the nappy bucket with nappy solution, fix the steriliser up for bottles and start to prepare a meal. Still little Christine would not settle down so I ran out to the chemist for some gripe mixture, and gave her that. I gave Harold a drink, as he was beginning to feel better. Then Karl came home from school looking lost and in a daze. I eventually sorted everyone out and at long last Christine went to sleep and I rolled into bed at midnight.

The next day, the baby was so fast asleep that it was nearly lunch time before she woke up. I kept looking at her to make sure she was still breathing. However it all ended well and Jeannette and Karl now have three children, all grown up, and three grandchildren too.

At home, Harold and I had reached a plateau; all our children were married, in their own homes, following their careers, and raising their own children.

Marjorie and John decided to buy a holiday cottage in Blaenau Ffestiniog, North Wales. It was only about an hour's run from the Wirral, and they spent weekends and holidays there with their three girls. It was in the Snowdonia area, with beautiful views, and in fact most of the family spent some holidays there.

In the 1980's Marjorie's husband John, had decided he would like to become a minister in the Church of England. He was working as an accountant, and had done a Lay Readers' course. He applied, and all seemed to go well towards being accepted. Then he had to spend a week at the Bishops' selection centre, where one is closely studied by learned people who decide if one is acceptable. Finally the answer came, that he was not accepted. (At that time lots applied and were rejected.) This was a great blow to John and Marjorie. He had told his firm he could be leaving, and also his friends, and now he had to go back cap-in-hand. As this was too much, he decided to try for a job running a post office, but as neither of them had worked in post offices, they didn't get very far with that.

Then he decided to buy a shop, and they ended up in Horwich, Bolton, with a small general shop, and their family moved to Horwich. It is a lovely country area outside Manchester. Harold helped them with the move, and all went well for a time. However, the stress had an adverse effect on their marriage. Judith would only be about 2 years old then.

Eventually they did split up and sold the shop. John went to live in the cottage in Wales while Marjorie continued to live in Horwich and her career progressed well.

The Grandchildren

As the years roll on and all my children have had children of their own; the grandchildren ranged quite close in ages. At various times such as birthdays and holidays we would all meet up.

I loved playing with the grandchildren. I would go upstairs with them and we would play make-believe games. I had a box of dressing up clothes. It was so rewarding, joining in the play and watching the interaction of the children.

I recall one day when they were about 2 to 7 years old, they decided to play at 'weddings'. Sarah at 7 was to be the bride. Hazel at 4 said she was to be the 'broom' and Ruth at 5 said she was to be the 'prime minister'. Christine who was 3 or 4 said she would be the nanny and have the 'bissies'. That was because I always carried Bismag tablets for indigestion! They proceeded with a white lace curtain on Sarah's head with little James who was 2, holding it at the back.

They are precious moments to remember.

Christine, Hazel, Ruth, Sarah
James, Judith, Heidi, Joseph

Another time we were at Marjorie's house with her children Sarah, Ruth and Judith. Ruth had been given a post office box for Christmas with all the paper money, stamps and books a post office uses. So they proceeded to set up this post office and I had to be the customer. Now Ruth did all the pension books and Sarah had the library. Judith was having a nap but I borrowed her little pink basket pram with a tiny doll to fit it. I knocked on the post office 'door' and explained that I needed my pension to get food for the baby. I started looking through the books in the 'library'

E.A.Pierce June 2008

with Sarah, enjoying the game. When Ruth handed over my money I was showing her the baby and she said to me,

"Nanny, was your baby an accident?"

Well, I collapsed laughing onto the bed. They both said,

"You're spoiling the game now."

Children are so innocent and rich!

Just a couple of the many games we played. It was so useful as their mums and dads could have a good natter together and catch up on all the latest news. The day usually ended with a 'nanny bath' where all the grandchildren would pile into the bath and play together. I would then scrub and dry each one in turn and so much fun was had.

When I went to Jeannettes's each week the children really looked forward to their 'nanny bath' before bed. Heidi still remembers those days and reminded me of it recently.

Baby Christine with Edith, Jeannette, Joyce and Marjorie, outside Jeannette's house in Blackburn

The End of an Era

It was the beginning of December 1981, when I had an afternoon off, and I was making some Christmas cards for the grandchildren. A knock came to my front door, and when I opened it, the traveller from Harold's firm, along with his secretary (Mrs Lappine) were standing there. I looked at them in a puzzled way, wondering why, and he said,

"Can we come in?"

"Yes but why?"

I asked, as they came into the living room. Mrs. Lappine burst into tears, and they said,

"We have some very sad news for you."

My reply was,

"It can't be Harold – his dinner is in the oven!"

But it was. Apparently the office boy had been up to his office, and knocked on his door, with no reply, so left it a while. Then he went up again, and still there was no answer. When the traveller for the firm came in, the boy went up to him and told him he had been twice up to see Mr. Pierce, with no answer. So he and Mrs. Lappine went up together and as they went in, found Harold slumped over his desk, dead. The police were called in, and an ambulance took him to hospital. He was declared dead on arrival, and later a post mortem proved a massive heart arrest.

It was such a tragedy. He was 64, and looking forward to retirement, which would have taken place the next week.

I then had to ring the girls, as they were all married by now, and living in different parts of the country.

It seemed almost unbelievable – as Harold left for work that morning he seemed fit and well, and jolly.

He had said to me,

"I'll be going now, have a good day."

He gave me a kiss and I said,

"You have a good day too."

Then by evening there was nothing. I couldn't even visit him in hospital. I kept thinking I was having a bad dream and would wake up, and be normal again. But no.

The family arrived, all very shocked, and we had to make arrangements for his funeral. To start with, the next day, Marjorie and Jeannette came with me to the Registry Office, in town. Being December, it was snowing. The death certificate had to be picked up, and specially printed out. Jeannette went to get it, and took it to the right department for printing out.

During this time, Marjorie and I stayed in the car, in the Registry Office car park. Here I must say, life still goes on! Whilst we were sitting there, feeling so terribly sad, a large grey car drew in, very old and scratched, with the tyres quite low, which was concerning as there was by now a few inches of snow. Then out of this car came a mother first, then a youngish girl (who looked about seven months pregnant), followed by a young lad chewing gum, and then the driver, who was probably the girl's father. They all walked into the Registry Office, obviously for the younger two to get married.

So, we still waited for Jeannette to come, then, about half an hour later, the doors opened, and out came the bride and groom. Also coming across the car park in the snow was a man with a camera and a big black case. The wedding group all stood in a row as the camera man took their photographs with a Polaroid.

Ten minutes later he was showing the family their wedding pictures. The bride at the front seemed quite proud of her bump, and as she held the picture, it fell to the ground in the snow. She picked it up, wiped it on her dress, and passed it round while the dad paid the camera man his money.

The family then all piled back into the old car; the bride was sitting on the groom's knee to fit them all in, and the tyres sank down into the snow. There followed some spluttering and screeching to get that car started. However they finally drove off, and Jeannette came out with the documents.

The day of the funeral approached and passed. Life had to continue. Marjorie and John had this shop in Horwich now, so had to get back to open the shop. Joyce and Jim had to go back to Ashton-U-Lyne, where he was teaching, and they had their two children. Jeannette and Karl had to get back to Blackburn as they were teaching around that area.
I was now on my own, in Liverpool. Even my sisters and brother had moved on.

Harold and I had started to make plans for when he retired, and Marjorie said,

> "You can't stay here on your own."

So I said,

> "I will move near to you, but not live with you. I have had a wonderful life, and will not dream of interrupting your lives."

So the wheels went into motion, to sell my house and move to Horwich near Marjorie.
At that time, the largest snowfall in years was recorded. Everywhere was thick with snow.
Harold's car had been brought back from his works, and whilst I could drive, I had never had full use of the car. I did borrow it

occasionally, but he always drove the long distances, and as I was the passenger, never took a great deal of notice of the routes we went.

While all the house negotiations were going on, I was invited to go and stay at Jeannette's for a couple of days. I was going on the train, and as I was locking my front door in Lynwood Gardens, my next door neighbour, Dick, came and saw me with my suitcase and said,

"Where are you off to?"

I told him I was going to Jeannette's, and he said,

"Why don't you use the car?"

"I can't get it in or out of the garage."

(It was quite difficult down the side of the house, with an awkward turn at the end.)

"I will get it out and put it back for you."

I still hesitated.

"Go and get the keys!"

He drove the car out of the garage and told me to get in. Very timidly I did, and when I got to the main road, I wasn't sure of the way! I had never had to do it on my own before! I did get the map out and followed it. I finally arrived at Jeannette's, and it was still snowing. Jeannette came out and said,

"You've come by car!"

"Dick made me!"

"Well good on Dick!"

I had a nice few days with them, but then Marjorie said,

> "Will you come over to me from Jeannette's, instead of going back to Liverpool?"

So I agreed, but that was my next obstacle! I had to learn how to cross country from Blackburn to Horwich. No main roads like in Liverpool, and of course all the local names were foreign to me. Jeannette did offer for Karl to escort me in their car, but I refused.

> "I have to depend on myself now."

She told me to go to the Preston roundabout, then take the road to Chorley. So I set off, and came to the roundabout, with the snow like curtains all round the car. I saw the sign to Bolton one way, and Chorley the other. As I had never heard of Chorley before, and thought that Marjorie's shop was in the Bolton area, and cars were coming up behind me, I made a decision to follow the Bolton sign. Little did I know, but it took me over the moors to Winter Hill, through Blackrod. I know it well now, but then, the wind was howling, the snow falling, deep drops each side of me and not another car in sight! The tears were running down my face. The two reservoirs were both frozen solid, and I thought,

> "If I go over the edge, that's both of us gone!"

It was a selfish thought, but I was feeling low. Anyway, I put the car into 3rd gear and drove on. How I found my way to the shop, I still don't know, but I did. When I told Marjorie the way I had come, she told me all the traffic had been stopped at Horwich from taking that route because of the weather – no wonder I hadn't seen another car!
But I made it!

Moving from Liverpool to Horwich didn't take very long. Marjorie and John followed up the houses for sale, as they were living there. I gave them a specification for the type I could cope with. It had to have an easy drive in, not on a slope, with a small garden. Eventually they found this one, fitting the bill perfectly. It only took two months to sell my house and buy this one, with very little difference in cost. Harold had left everything in order. He was so good. The time came to move in to Bond Close in Horwich, and I now had to learn my way around the neighbourhood.

Finding My Own Way

I wanted to go to see my Auntie Amy, my Dad's sister. We had been keeping an eye on her as she was on her own. Harold was very good to her, and she was lost when he died – in fact she only lived six months after. She lived in Knotty Ash in Liverpool, and had known Ken Dodd as a little boy, telling jokes on the stage in the local community hall.

I went fairly early. Again, I had to get the map out, and follow towards Wigan, pick up the M58, then follow from Fazakerly to Knotty Ash – a new route to me. She was so pleased to see me, and we had lunch together, then the time seemed to disappear. I set off for home to Horwich, and all was well until I had to come off the motorway, and find the side road towards Wigan. It was raining, and cars were behind me, so I didn't want to hesitate too much. The roundabout included the M6 North and South, so I carried on round, and found myself back on the motorway, with big signs for Blackpool and Preston!

It was now 10pm at night, and dark again, and I felt so lost! I decided I must get off this motorway at the next junction, wherever it took me. It was for Standish. I followed all the signs I understood, and eventually did arrive back to Bond Close.

I opened the front door, and the lights wouldn't go on! As I walked in the light bracket was dangling down. I thought I had had burglars – but no. I had left my bedroom window open and it was a very wet and windy day. The wind had caught the cock-loft lid at the top of the stairs and blown it right out, and it was lying on the floor. I had to get the step ladder out of the garage at the side of the house, (it was now 11pm) and carry the cock-loft lid up the ladder to put it back in the loft ceiling, then get a new lamp bulb to fit in before I could go to bed.

I started to feel sorry for myself, and then I decided it was only self-pity; no-one else would even know of my plight! Better just get on with it!

When I had worked in the hospital, I watched the W.R.V.S., and all the good voluntary work they did. So one morning after breakfast, I was feeling sad and tearful, as one does after a bereavement. Suddenly I thought of the W.R.V.S.; I had been helping with the shop and the children but sometimes, you need more. I rang the number in the phone book, and a lady answered. She asked me if I could drive, as they were desperate for drivers. I said I could, so she arranged to come and see me the next day. Her name was Lillian Rawlinson. She did a tremendous amount of work for the W.R.V.S., opening new clubs, helping the blind and disabled, organizing blood donors' evenings, where tea was served to donors after they had given blood. I soon got very involved.

In Horwich there was an office set up where we received charity clothes, and sold them or gave them to the needy. Another charity was set up for men or women who were just released from prison. They were given vouchers for clothes to get them started, and they came to the W.R.V.S. with their vouchers. Another venture was helping at the court side rooms. Couples who were separating, towards a divorce, met up with their children, and the W.R.V.S. supplied refreshments. I found that one rather sad, but all these projects made a difference to the lives of people in need.

One big achievement was to buy an ambulance, because moving disabled folks to and fro became more difficult using our cars.

We held a very big auction. It was a mighty effort, hiring a room and collecting large and small items. It was interesting and exciting, and we reached our target! Of course, driving it and getting wheel chairs on and off took an ambulance driver's skill, so we advertised for someone. I still sorted out the transport for our blind and disabled club.

Next, I took on helping with the dinner we provided at the club. One lady was responsible for the savoury, and I did the sweet. They all enjoyed those days out, and it relieved the boredom from just sitting at home.

We also took them on days out, and even occasional week's holidays. That was hard work, but very satisfying. Our Headquarters owned a holiday apartment in the Isle of Wight, and during those years, the voluntary workers could go on holiday. It was beautiful there.

The C.H.A

After Harold died, it took me time to face going to church, listening to the organ, but eventually I did, and I was introduced to Anne and Sally. Sally had just lost her husband at about the same time, so we latched on to each other, and did lots of things together. She joined the W.R.V.S., then also did Anne. Anne was a hiker, and belonged to the C.H.A (Countrywide Holiday Association) and encouraged me to join the local branch, which I did.

The C.H.A had walks arranged every Wednesday and Saturday; and each Tuesday evening there was a social get-together. I think the Saturday walkers were younger – they were the ones who were usually working in the week – and they did lots more miles!

They had the booklets one needed with all the information on the various walks each week. Each walk had a leader who led the walks and arranged any stops and a lunch break. Everyone carried lunch and flasks in rucksacks. You could choose to do an 'A', 'B' or 'C' walk. The 'A's would walk further and higher - about 10 miles, the 'B's about 8 miles, and the 'C's sometimes went part way by transport, and we all met up for lunch.

Out on a C.H.A hike

As time went on, every member was in turn elected to lead a walk. Many were familiar with the area around Bolton. I had now been out with the walkers a number of times and loved it. Then when we were issued with the new booklet, my name was down to lead one of the walks! As I keep saying, I was new to Horwich, and all the set route of the walk was foreign to me. So my friend Anne said,

> "The Sunday before that date, I will show you the route. We can take some sandwiches with us, and go round it."

So the Sunday arrived, and we set off. Much to my surprise, she brought a plastic bag, with some small empty paint cans, to put at the side of each style we had to climb over. It was up round Rivington in the heart of the countryside. Then we walked about half way and decided to have our sandwiches. By now it was getting towards twilight, and there were very few people about. We walked on a bit further, then she said,

> "I'm not so sure of this part now. We had better turn back."

However, after a couple more turns, we were lost, with no-one around now to ask. Just as we were getting worried, we saw one of the paint cans by a style, and were so relieved to follow them back!

I never had another chance to cover the second half of the walk that week. So the day arrived, we assembled at the meeting place, most arriving by car, and started the walk.
I started the walk quite confidently until we stopped for the lunch break. When we were ready for off, one of the blokes came to me and said,

> "Are we going now?"

I think he guessed I didn't know the way. He was a joking type, quite entertaining at the socials. Well he soon could tell I didn't have a clue, and pointed my shoulder to the way I had to go, over the stiles. It turned out quite funny, and when we were safely back, he collected a bunch of pretty weeds and said,

> "So much for your effort!"

Later, another year, I did manage to lead a couple of walks over the Wirral. We went by coach to the starting point, and it collected us from the destination. They were both very successful walks, over the sand dunes with beautiful sea views and on lovely sunny days.

When going on these walks, you had little stops to view the area, and found yourself then talking to another person, and became familiar with all the groups. They all had different tales to tell, with all their different careers and families.

A New Start

I had been in the C.H.A for four years when I met up with a man named John Watson. He was in his late 70's, and as we walked, he was complaining about people coming to this area at weekends, and yachting on Belmont Reservoir, spoiling the peacefulness. He was a native born and bred in the Horwich/Bolton area. I of course came from Liverpool, so I argued with him, saying that lots of those folks work hard all week, and are entitled to enjoy the countryside as well as him, at the weekend.

The argument became quite heated, so I thought he would have walked ahead and joined the others, but he didn't, and when we ended the walk he said to me,

> "Would you like to come to the modern sequence dance with me tonight?"

You can imagine I was taken aback, and replied,

> "I only have very little knowledge of sequence dancing, and also after all this walking, I'll be tired."

A couple of weeks on, he asked me again! So I started going, and I learned more and more about dances – and John.

He had been widowed for about ten years. Before retirement he had been a draughtsman in steam engineering, and pertaining to the machinery in the cotton mills. Latterly he had taught at Bolton College.

We began having walks and outings together. I didn't say much to my family for a while, because I thought he was a bit old then, and I always said when Harold died,

"I never want to go through that again, and I could never replace him."

But the years move on, and the brain heals.

John and I had been friends for nearly a year, when it was my birthday. He asked me what I would like for a present; as I didn't really know his circumstances money-wise, I wasn't sure what to ask for.

We arranged to go to Bury for a meal, and we were passing a jeweller's shop. He stopped and looked in the window, and said to me,

"Anything in here you would like?"

I decided on a small bracelet, so we went in. Then, as I was looking at a card of bracelets, he said to the assistant,

"Bring out that card of rings."

I said,

"Oh no!"

"Try one on."

"I'll just have one of these bracelets."

Then the assistant said to me,

"If I was being offered a ring, I would jump at the offer!"

So I came out with a beautiful diamond ring, and believe me, I couldn't tell anyone at first!

One day we were walking hand in hand up by Rivington, when a car drove past. It was Marjorie and her family in it! The children had recognised me. I saw it, but John didn't, but the next moment the car had turned back, and I had to introduce them to each other.

A week or so later, I was at Joyce's when her husband Jim said,

"I think your mother is wearing a new ring!"

After that, John became familiar with all the family. He was now nearing his 80's, but still quite tough and daring. We continued walking and going to the sequence dancing. I had no intention of getting married again; I just wanted to stay friends with no commitment.

I arranged to have a holiday at the cottage in Blaenau Ffestiniog with Marjorie and her family during the summer. As the time got nearer, John said to me,

"Could I not join you?"

I did ask Marjorie if he could come, and she said he would have to sleep downstairs on a Z-bed. He was happy with that, so we all went. It is a beautiful spot in Snowdonia.

One morning Marjorie had gone out with the girls to do the shopping. John was in the bathroom getting washed and shaved, and I was washing the breakfast dishes and tidying the living room, with the radio on. I was listening to the news, and heard the announcement of Prince Andrew and Sarah Ferguson's marriage. It sounded exciting.

Very soon after, Marjorie arrived back with the children, and John came walking down the stairs at the same time. I walked into the hall and said,

"The wedding has just been announced!"

Immediately, John said to me,

"I thought you were keeping it a secret yet."

"It's the ROYAL WEDDING!"

"No it's not, it's ours!"

I was just dumbfounded as he carried on and said,

"I have even booked that Italian village, Portmerion, for our honeymoon!!"

I couldn't believe what I was hearing, but all the family joined in and said why not?
When he did really ask me to marry him, I said,

"You could be dead before the day!"

"Charming! If I was struggling to walk or gasping for breath, I wouldn't even ask you."

"Well I didn't want to go through the trauma of bereavement again."

"Well you know me now, so I'm sure it wouldn't be that different."

So I accepted, and we had a very nice wedding with all the families. He came to live in my house, as it was more convenient.

Edith and John

Marjorie's New Start

It so happened that Marjorie had decided to leave her John, and liked my John's bungalow. We had it valued, and Marjorie took out a mortgage on it, and moved in with her girls. They had sold their shop by now, and John went to live in the cottage in Blaenau Ffestiniog.

Marjorie applied for a new post and became a tutor at the Bolton Royal Hospital. She already had a B.A. through the Open University, and after a couple of years the hospital management seconded her to do a teaching qualification and then a further degree at Manchester, where she attained a Masters degree in Complementary Medicines. She then wrote three degree courses, which were validated and used. She then became a senior lecturer at the University of Central Lancashire in Preston. Her ex-husband John also did a masters degree in Business Studies, which he went on to teach at Edge Hill University.

So Marjorie was living with the three girls in the bungalow in Horwich, and working full time. Sarah was a teenager, and getting boyfriend-orientated, whilst moving towards getting a settled job. At an interview with the careers officer, Sarah said she didn't want an indoor boring job, so it was arranged for her to sit an exam in relation to doing an apprenticeship in engineering. Marjorie asked me to take her in my car as she was working, to make sure she got there on time.

The exam was at Hick Hargreaves Headquarters, and there were fifty boys and ten girls. Well those boys all looked so smart – their mothers must have got them ready! The exam was to last four hours, and when I picked her up later, she was saying it was "quite hard". The boys were all saying how easy it was – all bravado!

In the meantime, Sarah obtained a job at a pipe works, near the Bolton bus terminus. She settled into this for a time, then one day she was messing about with the lads, and one of the large pipes got broken. She came to me and said,

> "Nan, I can't tell my mum, but I might get the sack, and she will be so cross!"

I did give her a talking-to, and she heard no more, until the next week. She received word to attend the business office in Bolton, and she got a bit worried, thinking it would be the sack. In great trepidation she had to go. She related the incident to me later – and she was good at imitating people.

> "There were four huge business men, and I was there expecting the sack. One of them said, 'Do you remember sitting the exam at Hick Hargreaves? Well from the results, we chose ten boys and two girls, and you are one of the girls.'"

He went on to tell her how she was to serve her time, and what was expected of her. At that moment, the relief of not getting the sack hit her. She burst into tears! He said,

> "Just stop that! You are in a man's world now!"

Sarah went to the loco works and started her training. She came top in most of the projects and then went on to Bolton University to do design engineering. When she went to the end of year ball, the lads said,

> "You don't half scrub up well!"

They were so used to seeing her in her overalls and oil!

As the years rolled on, she married and had two beautiful children, so was at home for a while. Trying to get back into engineering was difficult, as the firms didn't want to know about maternity leave, or sick children – many of them didn't even have toilets for women! So she now works in a solicitor's office.

Marjorie's second child, Ruth, started showing signs of being musical from very early years. When Sarah started learning to play the piano, Ruth was only 3, and she wanted to do the same. At first the music teacher said children that young do not have the necessary co-ordination, and wouldn't include her in the sessions, so Marjorie gave her some early lessons. Later, she asked the teacher to listen to what she could do, and when she actually listened to Ruth's playing, she at last agreed it was not too early! Ruth soon overtook Sarah, and is now a beautiful pianist. She was in the Junior Bolton Orchestra for a while.

Ruth had reached teenage-hood when Marjorie took them on a camping holiday in France. There, she met a Scottish boy, and became friendly with him, so went up to Edinburgh to live. She was there eight years, and that friendship, as well as a couple more, came and went. She moved back down to Bolton, and met up with Pete, whom she already knew from before moving up to Edinburgh, and married him. She now has two lovely boys of her own.

Judith, the youngest of Marjorie's three girls, was quite a placid child. She works in middle management for Salford Council, and has settled down to life with Paul, and is very happy.

When Marjorie was tutoring at Bolton, (at the time her marriage was sliding), she was under the doctor with query gall bladder problems, inflammation and kidney stone. The doctor decided he would operate on her. She arranged everything for the children, and sorted everything out for whilst she would be in hospital. I was also around to help. On the morning of her operation I had been to the florist to order some flowers to be delivered to the ward after her operation. It was a Thursday morning, so I decided I would be better still going to Jeannette's so I would be occupied. Marjorie had lost a lot of weight and I was worried about her.

As I walked through the door at Jeannette's, she asked me,

"Have you had a phone call from the hospital about Marjorie?"

"Why? Should I have had one?"

"They are not now doing the operation!"

Immediately I burst into tears and said,

"They must have found cancer! I'm going to the hospital!"

Well, Jeannette, always very down to earth, said to me,

"Now just sit down and have a cup of tea. That is your opinion, and you don't know!"

So I did as I was told, and waited for more news.

Then at 12 noon, Marjorie herself came on the phone, so upset. What had happened, and what I didn't know, was that the inspectors over the schools of nursing had been into Bolton hospital prior to this operation. This doctor was known to be a very good surgeon, and known for getting the operations through on time. The criticism from the inspectors to the school was that the teaching was very good, but they were using junior pupils for major surgery, and should have senior nurses or staff nurses for that standard. Now when the doctor heard this, Marjorie was in the side ward. He visited her and said,

"How am I expected to carry out my work if you are taking nurses off me?"

"Doctor, I am not the allocations officer, and at this moment, I am a patient!"

she replied.

He went away, and after she had had all the pre-med treatment, and was ready to go to theatre, he came back.

> "If I don't have the nurses, I can't do your operation, so you can get dressed and go home!"

She was so shocked to be used as a scapegoat. The school of nursing were up in arms, took Marjorie back to their offices, and a meeting was called. I think the doctor in question had to face a meeting of doctors, and had to apologise. So later, Marjorie was taken home in a terrible state.

I left Jeannette's, and went straight to Marjorie's house. She had arrived home, and was explaining the whole story to me, when a knock came to the door. It was the boy from the florist's saying,

> "Does Marjorie Curtis live here? I have been all over the bloody hospital looking for her with these flowers."

Marjorie shouted,

> "And I've been over the bloody hospital too!"

I had forgotten all about the flowers!

Marjorie was in such a low state, John, her husband, rang the vicar of the church. I was still with her when the curate arrived – it would be about 7pm by now. This curate was great. He talked to her, and then said,

> "Do you mind if I lay my hands on your head and pray?"

> "Do what you like," said Marjorie, "I don't care if I live or die!"

At this point, I decided to go home, but this curate (yet another 'John') went every night and laid his hands on her and prayed, for a week, until Marjorie was recovering from all that trauma.

Eventually, another doctor came to the house and said he was going to take over Marjorie's case. He was going to do x-rays, and give her some treatment. About six months later she had fresh x-rays taken, and he compared them to the earlier ones. He told her all the inflammation had healed, and the gall bladder had healed. She would not now need an operation. That is faith healing indeed!

We go through these testing times with hope and prayer, and rise again. Marjorie recovered, and settled down to life. She and John separated, and as I have mentioned, eventually she did her masters degree and moved on to become a senior lecturer at Central Lancashire University.

More About the Family

Joyce and her husband Jim had two children, Hazel and James (junior). Hazel was a very active little girl, very lovable, but also quite determined! She did quite well at school; she attained a B.Sc. at Edge Hill University, Maghull, outside Liverpool. At first she trained to be a teacher, but later she decided teaching was not for her. After a couple of years in the hospitality industry, managing bars, she applied for a position in the civil service, dealing with pensions for the M.O.D., and has progressed well. She did have a sad set-back in that the boyfriend she was dating suddenly had a heart attack and died whilst in the gym. It was so unexpected, and it took time to come to terms with. She has now settled down with Martin, and is happily living in Surrey.

All the grandchildren have participated in musical activities and played various instruments but, in each of the three families, it is the second child who has inherited the musical talent from Harold.

Ruth showed musical awareness from very early on; she would ask for records to be played when she could barely talk, and when Sarah was learning to play she would cover her ears with her hands and plead with her mum to make Sarah stop! Ruth learned to play the piano to a high standard and still enjoys having a go occasionally, sometimes playing duets with her mum.

Heidi has made music her career and works within the church as a musical director as well as teaching private piano pupils.

James started playing the violin when he was six. A friend at school had an under-developed hand and her mum was advised that learning the violin would be good exercise and therapy. She asked around and found that the Suzuki violin teacher would come to school if a few children wanted to learn. They started off with little tiny violins which they learned to play by ear, marching round the room.

A few weeks later, one of their neighbours was putting on a concert to raise money for charity and asked all the local children to take part. James had only had a few lessons but played variations of 'Twinkle, twinkle little star' on his tiny violin, to great applause. One of the other neighbours in the audience played in the Halle Orchestra, and he said afterwards that James definitely had talent. He continued to learn, took part in many musical activities in school, church and festivals and passed grade eight when he was 16. He also sang with the Manchester Cathedral Voluntary Choir as a boy.

James was a quieter child, and very contented. He worked well and studied, and attained a place in Newcastle University, in the medical school. After qualifying, he decided to specialise in Orthopaedics, where he is an M.R.C.S., and loves the work.

When the two children were growing up, Jim their father was Deputy Head at Two Trees High School in Denton, and Joyce was teaching maths at Aquinas College. Everyone was doing quite well when Jim suddenly took a serious illness. It seemed to involve his immune system, and he went into intensive care during this crisis. It took a couple of years to recover, and he was advised not to go back into teaching, with all the stress. He eventually obtained a job with the Civil Service, and life settled down again.

Jeannette and her husband Karl went to live in Blackburn, both with teaching posts. Jeannette gave up work when they had Christine, the first of their three children. Joseph, their youngest was about two years old when Karl was not so well, and decided to give up teaching. They then bought a local shop, a general grocery and confectionery business, which did reasonably well, and they had it for a few years. They were also involved with the evangelistic church, where Karl was Church Warden, and Jeannette played guitar in the music group. It was always nice and jolly to join in when visiting.

After a few years, Jeannette returned to teaching, and they moved out of the shop, and then later down to Cheshire, for Karl to take a degree at Elim Bible College in Nantwich. A year after completing his degree, Christine also attained a place there, and likewise got a B.A. in Theology. She also met Eddie there, whom she married, and they now have three lovely children.

When Jeannette and Karl moved down to Nantwich, they joined the Elim Church. In time, Christine and Heidi decided they wanted to be baptised. Karl's parents at that time lived in Leyland (near Preston) and I was in Horwich, so Jeannette asked if I could pick up Karl's parents en route down to Nantwich, for the service at the Elim church. I had my husband John still alive then, so we called for Karl's parents who were also called Edith and John!

It was a beautiful morning. Edith had made quite a picnic of buns, cakes and flasks of coffee. So we set off down the M6 and arrived in good time.

The baptisms were held in the swimming pool, in the grounds of the Bible College in Nantwich. The sunshine was blazing through all the windows, scintillating on the water. Then one by one, each candidate was taken into the water, blessed, and fully immersed. As each one came out, a hymn was sung, with Jeannette playing the guitar, at the edge of the pool. Then each one stood separately and gave a testimony about what the baptism meant to them. It was so wonderful to watch – it brought a tear to your eye. Then later everyone joined in refreshments and chatted together.

A number of year later, Joseph, Jeannette and Karl's youngest, was being baptised. It was in a baptistery pool in a hall this time. In that gap of time, my eldest granddaughter, Sarah, had married, and now had a little boy, named Benjamin. He came with us to Joseph's baptism. We were all sitting round the pool, watching the procedure. Benjamin, now aged 2 ½ years old, jumped up when Joseph was fully immersed, and ran off saying,

"I don't want to go next. I've had a bath!"

We did laugh, but we also experienced another really lovely day.

Heidi, Jeannette's middle child, as I've said, was very musical. She studied for her B.A. in Music and Theology at London School of Theology, and works as Director of Music at a church in Berkhamsted, Hertfordshire, as well as several other posts teaching music, and working for the Music and Worship Foundation, encouraging quality music in churches across the country.

Their youngest child, Joseph had just reached his 'A' levels, when he started to feel ill. He was very listless and found a lump on his neck. Jeannette took him to the doctor, and he was sent for tests. The results came through – it was Hodgkin's Lymphoma cancer. As you can imagine we were all very shocked.

He had chemotherapy, followed by radiotherapy. He was rushed into Christies Hospital from time to time when his blood count got too low, for blood transfusions. Jeannette had to learn how to give him daily injections to help his system cope. We were so worried about him, and many churches were praying for him, as we all were. Gradually he regained his health; he was a good strong patient. He is now working in Barclays bank in Guernsey, along with giving a lot of time and service to the youth groups in his church.

Sisters and Brothers

I will now slip back in time to follow the events and movements of my sisters and brother. In the 50's and 60's, Liverpool had a great upsurge. The government wanted to improve the areas that were overcrowded, and rebuild some of the city to increase work opportunities. So, new housing developments were started; first in Kirkby, then Speke and Skelmersdale, Runcorn and Huyton. Factories and business industrial areas were built, and communities were encouraged to move out of the city. It was called the 'overspill'. It gave hundreds of families a fresh start. My brother and family was the first to move, to Knowsley, near where the Safari park is now, to a brand new house outside Liverpool. They settled down and the children did very well. Sadly, Reg died, only a few years ago.

Laura, my eldest sister, and her husband Allan had a lovely daughter Anne. They settled in Fazakerley. They were Jehovah's Witnesses. When Anne grew up she met and married Jon, who was in the same religion. They decided to train as missionaries, and were allotted to go to Chile, South America for a number of years. Then eventually Anne was pregnant and they came back to England to live on the South Coast. Laura and Allan were now at retirement age, so moved off to live in Runcorn where they ended their days in 1984-6.

Ida bought a house and took our parents to live with her (in the 1960's) until they started with serious illnesses and died in the years 1960/1, as I mentioned earlier. So Ida then wanted to move into a little bungalow, in a more rural place called Melling, just outside Liverpool. She still travelled to work to Sefton General Hospital each day. Ida was always independent - she went on holidays abroad long before most people could afford to, being still single and having a career. She also represented the Royal College of Midwives on conferences in such places as Madrid and Czechoslovakia. She was always very good with the nephews and nieces, but now these children were older and were becoming independent themselves.

Before Harold died, Rose, Arthur, Harold and I had arranged a holiday with the C.H.A, on the Isle of Man. The C.H.A. arranged group holidays where everyone went on walks together, played games and had entertainments. Ida asked me if she could join us, as it was a mixed holiday, and we said of course. This was one of the hottest summers recorded.

We arrived at Douglas by boat, and went on to the C.H.A. guest house. When we reached the place, we were invited in to a side room, and sitting on his own in here was a gentleman, who, we learned, had come from Nelson for the week. The weather was so hot, all the folks at the C.H.A. were bathing at the front in the sea. The host for the week was sent for to come and settle us in, and while we waited, we chatted to this chap, whose name was Gilbert. As we parted to go to our rooms, he said to us,

"Can I sit with you at tea time, now we have met?"

After tea, we had dancing and games, so Gilbert really became friendly, and with Ida being on her own, they palled up.

It was a coach trip out the next day, so Ida and Gilbert sat together, and there began a romance! He was on his own. His wife had died two years previous, with diabetes, when she was just one year off retirement.

Edith, Arthur
Harold, Ida, Gilbert,
and Rose

Ida and Gilbert were married the following Christmas. Ida sold her bungalow at Melling and moved to Colne where they bought a bungalow together. When Ida married Gilbert, she became step-mother to his children; Pat, the eldest and David were already married with families and Alan was married to Maureen just a few weeks before.

Gilbert was very good at painting, mainly landscapes so Ida became interested and has produced quite a number of really good paintings and drawings. They spent over 10 years travelling about and helping with the grandchildren. Harold and I then had a different area to go and visit and we became familiar with Colne and the surrounding places.

They were married for eleven very happy years before Gilbert died after suffering from a cancer. On the day of his funeral, Marjorie, Jeannette and I arranged to go. We knew which church the service was at but were not quite sure where it was, so intended to call in at Ida's first. The journey took longer than we thought so we decided to find the church first as time was going on and we didn't want to be late.

It seems that it was the custom in Colne to take the coffin to the church the day before and leave it open until the funeral. The night before there had been a storm with heavy rain. The wind had been so strong, it had blown some of the glass out of the large window of this church. We drove around and found the church, we thought, and decided to check if it was the right place.

Marjorie walked into the dimly lit church and saw the window with a curtain blowing out. Gilbert was in his coffin which had the lid open and his hair was blowing in the wind. She ran out, quite scared, but we saw the funny side of it. There was a man in the garden repairing the damage from the storm.

The service went ahead and afterwards his daughter, Pat, had arranged for a meal at her home. We were to follow one of the cars to Pat's house. We had her address but the traffic was so busy that we lost them at a roundabout. After several tries and asking directions at a post office, we eventually arrived, although the family had all been wondering where we had gone!

The couple living in the bungalow facing Ida and Gilbert had become very friendly with them. They were Albert and Dorothy. She had latterly started with heart trouble, and Ida, being a nurse, advised Albert and helped them. Years later, when both Gilbert and Dorothy had died, Albert and Ida kept each other company. Then suddenly Albert asked her to marry him. He wasn't in good health himself then though, but she accepted. So Ida, having been single until 59, was married twice. She and Albert had about six happy years together. Ida is now in her 90's, in a nursing home after a serious illness.

That brings me to Gladys, my younger sister. Gladys married Bob in 1941. They settled down in Aintree near the race course. We could walk down the road and watch the races, including the Grand National, by the big gates at Melling Road. She had Irene, Brian and Ian, and a long while later had another little girl who died only weeks old. They had a few turmoils over the years, but kept on. Years later she had Hilary, followed by Gordon. They have all grown up now and are in responsible jobs.

During the war, Bob was away with the forces in England, and I will recall a small incident with Irene, the eldest. When she was born, Harold was away at war, and Gladys was still living with us at Rawcliffe Road. I helped Gladys and looked after Irene, and took her out quite a lot. She was like a doll between us, we loved her so much!

The day came as I have recounted, when Harold arrived back in England after 3½ years away; Irene was about 2½ years old then. That very morning, I was standing close to Harold, and we were chatting and laughing. Irene didn't like that. She pulled him by the trouser legs, and was trying to push him out saying,

"My auntie Edie, not yours!"

Much later, Gladys and Bob moved out to a nice house in Warrington. Bob died in the late 80's. She still lives there with Brian, her son who returned home from Johannesburg some years ago. Brian still visits his daughter Lara out there now. Lara is also married with a daughter herself.

Life with John

John Watson was a very outgoing person. When I married him in 1986, I didn't realize his potential. He never wanted to stop indoors even though he had turned 80! He was born in Bolton, and I think he knew every blade of grass! He would have his breakfast (a full English one every day), then say,

"Let's make sandwiches, and fill the flasks, and be off!"

So with rucksacks on, off we went even in the winter. As I keep saying, I was still relatively new to the areas, and sometimes when we went walking over the moors at Rivington, it was very icy. I used to think that if he had slipped and fallen, I would never have known my way down to get help. Well, that didn't happen, but we did have some hair-raising events! He was never timid about travelling paths that were prohibited or private.

One day we prepared to go for a walk and have lunch at a place called 'Old Rozins' – it was near Darwen. We went so far in the car, then hiked. John always had a strong walking stick, which did come in useful at times. So we parked the car and started to cross the fields. We came to a gypsy encampment. They had about six Rottweiler dogs chained to small wooden kennels, where we had to pass through. These dogs all started at once barking and baring their teeth, and the kennels were moving with them! I was so frightened! Then a big dray horse, dapple grey, came charging past us on its own. I wouldn't go back that way home!

We arrived at this very old public house, so we went in. It had little tiny lights. At first we couldn't see, until our eyes adjusted to the dimness. John went off to the toilet, and I heard a voice say,

"Is that Edith?"

I thought,

"I must be hearing things – no one knows me here."

Then it came again, and I peered across the darkness. I had heard right! One of the ladies in the W.R.V.S. who I worked with, named Marion, was there with her husband, mother, brother and his wife, all celebrating her mother's birthday. As we were having a little chat, John came walking in. Marion's brother stood up and walked towards John, held out his hand and said,

"Are you Mr. Watson?"

It was one of John's past pupils he had taught at Bolton College – Steam Engineering. He was working in Malaysia, and I think his wife was from those parts. They were home on a holiday. The mother said what a good teacher John was – her son had a marvellous job out there. What a coincidence!

I continued my voluntary work with the W.R.V.S. and we still walked with the C.H.A. every Wednesday. In fact John went out on his own walking quite often, in all weathers. I remember one evening; it was thunder and lightning, and the time had got to nearly 10pm and he hadn't returned. John was now well up in his eighties. I thought he must have tripped and fallen, amongst the trees. I was just about to go and ring the police, when he arrived back saying how wonderful it was watching the lightening, sheltering under a big tree!

I had a lovely neighbour next door – her name was Rhoda. When I first came to Horwich she was so good to me. She had her husband alive then. After he died, we became really good friends. She had two sons, David and Howard, and they visited her, and as she grew older, they supported and cared for her until she died. We also had formed a group of friends from Horwich Church, with Doris, Kath and Tom, Jean, June, and Anita. We had regular trips to the Amateur Dramatics shows, and for a time played cards and dominoes each Sunday evening, at the various houses.

John had only one sister who had never married. She worked with design and fashions in Bolton but had died before I met John. He also had a cousin named George whose wife was Ruth. George was more than a cousin as his father and John's father were brothers who had married two sisters. I think George was an engineer. John and his first wife, Dorothy, sadly did not have any successful pregnancies. They had only one little boy full term who was stillborn. John and George were very close and after Dorothy died George and Ruth looked after John and helped him in lots of ways. He was on his own for 10 years until we were married.

Now Ruth and George had three married daughters the same as me, and also eight grandchildren, like me. We all became very friendly, joined forces and visited each other. John was delighted to have the family connection and very proud to attend important events. Mind you, he had to learn and understand how to cope with children.

He and George had lovely tenor singing voices and George was in Smithills Church choir. John loved to go when my grandson James was singing in Manchester Cathedral. On one occasion, one of the adult choristers recognised John as his teacher from Bolton College. For a long time he thought that James was John's grandson as they both had the red hair.

E.A.Pierce June 2008

I have mentioned some of John's adventures; he always loved being out walking. One day he went off on his own when I was doing my W.R.V.S. duty. He decided to go near Worthington Lakes and after getting off the bus, he cut through a path where he tripped and fell. His glasses flew off and he caught his hand on a rough rock. Luckily a man walking nearby helped him up, found his glasses and went on his way. John's hand was bleeding so he decided to go home and walked back to the bus stop. When the bus came, he showed the driver his hand, and he could see that it was split right across the palm. The driver said that he needed to go to hospital so John travelled on that bus then had to change to another one to take him to the hospital.

When he arrived, they were amazed that no-one had called for an ambulance. They thought that a man half his age couldn't have travelled like that. However, at 7pm that evening I received a phone call from Bolton Hospital asking me to come and pick him up. He looked a right wounded soldier with 15 stitches across his hand, all bandaged up with a sling on. That was how I took him home. He made a remarkably quick recovery with no permanent damage and no infection setting in; he was very lucky!

Eventful Walks

We still belonged to the C.H.A. and John's name was on the list to lead a walk from Horwich to White Coppice, about four miles each way. He said,

> "I think we had better do a reccy (reconnoitre) on that walk, to be sure."

So the evening before, we set off about 5pm and took a snack with us, and a flask. We went in the car and left it by the reservoirs, and walked up a few steps leading into a field. It had about fifteen cows in it, all chewing away. We followed the paths and arrived at White Coppice without problems. We sat down, had our snack, then before going back, John said,

> "I will have a look at the cricket area, where the practice pen is."

It had a well known cricket club, and a place for refreshments during the day. It was evening now, and I think all had gone home for tea, as there was no-one about. I then walked on, along this path, and came to a beautiful landscaped garden. While I was admiring it, a border collie dog came up to me with its tongue lolling out, and panting. I was a bit uneasy, so gave it a pat and said,

> "Nice dog",

thinking it would go. But no! When John came down, as we set off back home, this dog would not leave us, and every time we passed a field of sheep, it went right down on its haunches, ready to charge, and every time it took a side path away from us, we thought it had gone home, but no! We even ran to get away from it, but it walked beside us all the way until we were nearing this field of fifteen cows.

This dog ran ahead into this field, and it set on all the cows. As we followed up, we couldn't believe the way it had disturbed the cows. The dog drove the cows to the other side of the field and must have run out at the far end, because as we walked into this field, we were now the only things moving around. Now, with no other way for us to go, and held in with barbed wire, the cows all came back heading towards us, tongues hanging out, and heads down! I said,

> "We are going to get killed!"

John had his big stick and an umbrella. He said,

"Take my stick, and I will have the umbrella."

We were surrounded by these cows, our backs to the wall, hitting out, shouting,

"Get back! Get back!"

One brown one caught John at the side, and he bashed it across its nose. We had to keep moving towards the steps, sideways, lashing out, with my legs getting weaker and weaker, until we made the gate by the steps. I nearly fell down the steps! There was no other person in sight, but guess what! There was the dog! Believe you me, I swore at it!
This time we hurried to the car, with the dog following us, and fell into the car, exhausted.

When the day came to lead the walk, those cows never even looked up! But I had a couple of nights waking up, and seeing those cows heading for us.

John had some very close friends who were farmers, and when we told them about it, they said we had indeed been in great danger. If I had slipped down, I would have been trampled to death. But again we were okay!

Life wasn't always so hectic – we did have some lovely 'normal' walks – it's just these unusual events that we remember more vividly.

Another time we went on holiday to visit the farm in Auchencairn, Dumfries. There were three brothers all on farms – this one in Auchencairn, one in Shrewsbury and the other one in Lockerby. John (yes, yet another 'John'!), the brother in Auchencairn always made us very welcome. Whilst we were there, my John had the map out and wanted to go to one of the small mountainous areas just beyond Dumfries, again a very quiet area.

We set off, and the start of this walk was through the dense woods, with lots of different paths. Being a true Girl Guide, I made some tracking signs with the branches – lots of arrows, then we came to a sort of fence, and as we touched it, it had a small electric current. We had to climb over this fence, and John said,

> "I'll go first."

> "Oh no! Don't leave me!" I said.

> "Well you go first."

> "I can't," I replied.

> "Make up your mind – someone has to move!"

So he went first, and we stepped into this area at the other side, up to our thighs in strong grass and heather. We proceeded to walk on and up, not an animal or a soul in sight. It was like being on the moon! We walked about half way up this hill, and not having a compass, didn't know exactly what direction, as it all looked alike. We sat down on our coats for a while and enjoyed the difference – a blue sky, and all high grass. However, when we started back down, we didn't have a clue where we had first climbed over that fence. We kept walking on round, and began to get worried, when suddenly I spotted my tracking signs! With great relief we headed back to the car.

Another small funny happening! John the farmer said to us never to go through the field with the bull in.

> "We have to get him out sometimes, and he's a bit hard even for us to handle!"

So we didn't dare.

E.A.Pierce June 2008

The next day while we were having tea, a message came through, that the bull had got out of the field and was loose! So John the farmer rushed out down the road. Coming along was a little boy of nine, with the bull on a rope, walking side by side, bringing it back! We never cease to wonder!

Another time we had booked a holiday in Llandudno, a glorious sunny week. On the Wednesday, we prepared for our usual trek; we walked from Llandudno towards Rhos-on-Sea, along the sea front. We came to the little Orme. At this side, a wall with a climbable rough front seemed okay, so we decide to try it. All went fine until getting to the very top, on the last step up, there was nothing to grip. The land sloped away and up, all grass. I stood on the last step with one foot, and to take the next step I would have to throw myself on to the sloping earth, and just nothing to grab! I looked back but couldn't turn back – so threw myself forward and was now lying on the slope. There was only short grass, and if I had slid back, I would have gone over the edge. John was up and struggling past me. I said,

"Help! I'm stuck!"

"I can't – I'm just edging my way," he replied.

So I had to dig my fingers into the grass and edge myself up the grassy slope until I could stand up. We then walked right over to the other side of the Orme. When we started to make our way down, a couple of hikers on the road saw us and shouted,

"What are you doing up there? Have you read this big notice on this wall?"

We carefully climbed down and looked at it. It said,

**"This Orme claims two lives every year.
KEEP OFF."**

But we made it, and walked back around the roadway, a safe path back to Llandudno!

The next year we decided to book a holiday on Anglesey. All these trips we really did enjoy, but John was never happy with a straightforward walk. We stayed in a caravan near the Menai Bridge. It had a sort of inlet to cross as you came out of the caravan park. Well, what a time we had this day! Starting off with rucksacks, boots, lunch and flasks, we had walked about two miles when we saw a sloped path going up, with a white gate, half open, at the bottom. We couldn't see beyond the path, but it seemed to be all fields, so John said,

"Let's try up this path."

So we proceeded up, and as we came to the top, it was like a disused airfield, and I said,

"We shouldn't be here."

"It's one that was used during the war, but it's derelict now."

So we continued to walk across, when suddenly we heard a small plane land in the distance. The far side of this area had barbed wire round, so we carried on. Then about five minutes later a huge Harrier jet plane started coming down. We were on the field about 100 yards from the landing strip, and we began to feel the draught, and John waved to the pilot. As it came nearer, we felt the vibration and John said,

"Quick, run!"

I turned and started to run back to the way we had come in, but I didn't see which way John ran.

As I was nearing the gate back to the main path, a small car came behind me. It stopped me and the man inside asked,

"What are you doing on this ground? Have you seen the large penalty notice at the front of this place?" (The penalty, we found out later, was huge!)

"No," I said, "I haven't seen any notice. The gate was open and I thought it was okay."

"You had someone with you. Where is he?"

"He went off in another direction."

I had to confirm we were only hikers innocently walking round that area, and after a while and some questioning, he let me go.

I then didn't know where John was, and it was nearly an hour before we met up. I called him a coward for leaving me to face the music!

We enjoyed the rest of the day, but on returning to the caravan, that stream I mentioned had grown to three times its size, and we had to cross it! We had to take our boots and socks off, and it was a toss up who was going in first, to find out how deep it was! Well we were just able to wade across – it was up to our thighs, so we went back all wet!

When we were driving back home, on the way, we decided to call in on John's friends, the farmers in Shrewsbury. Now the caravan we had been staying in belonged to another friend who lived in Bolton. David and Janet, the Shrewsbury farmer and his wife, had moved from Bolton a few years before. While we were having tea, we chatted about Anglesey and the caravan, and Janet asked,

"Is the name of the caravan owner 'Morris'?"

"Yes."

"We know that family very well! His wife was a bridesmaid to my daughter."

She then showed us the wedding photographs. It's a small world, isn't it?

Caravan Capers

One of my friends in Horwich, Doris, who originated from Liverpool, had a caravan on a plot of land in Pilling on the Fylde. Doris and George invited John and me to visit them there occasionally. One day when we were out walking with the C.H.A., another friend, Milly said to me,

> "A lady in our church has decided to let her caravan out for a week as part of the fundraising for the church."

They were having some repairs done and the congregation was making a big effort to pay for them. Normally these caravans were not allowed to be let out, but this lady had asked for special permission so that the money could go to the church. I rather liked the idea of a holiday in a caravan and decided I would ask if some of the grandchildren could come, and we could see Doris too as it was on the same plot of land.

John and I booked it. We took Jeannette's children, Christine (12), Heidi (9) and Joseph (6) and Judith (10) who is Marjorie's youngest. So Milly, who first suggested it, and four children with me and John all went. It was like a large bungalow and we turned the seating round at night for beds. John had a small compartment on his own and the rest of us fitted in around the main part.

One night there was an almighty bang, and Milly shot out of bed, thinking there had been a gas explosion. She woke me up, and together we went to see if we could find the cause of it. It turned out that Christine had fallen out of the bunk bed! There she was on the floor, still asleep, blissfully unaware of the panic she had caused!

The weather was lovely and the camp site had a swimming pool. The children could get changed and run down to the pool, although they were never allowed to go without one of us adults, and what a great time they had. We had a trip to Knott End, right on the coast and played in the sands.

At night we all sat round the table and played card games. The family who owned the caravan had bikes there and a croquet set to play on the grass. We made full use of everything. We went over to Doris's caravan and Jeannette and Karl came to visit us on the Wednesday. We all had such a good time; the children were reluctant to go home at the end of the week.

Each year they would say to me,

"Can we not go to that caravan holiday again?"

I did ask but it was only a one-off opportunity.

An Accident

When I first knew of Bolton, it was described as a dirty, smoky town because of all the mills and their tall chimneys all belching smoke. It was a great weaving area (like the song from the Houghton Weavers; *'If it wasn't for the weavers what would we do? We wouldn't have a bob-cap made of wool'*). It has the lakes and reservoirs needed for the cloth, with beautiful countryside and parks for walking. Today, since the industry has moved to China and other developing countries, the mills are used for other industries and many of the chimneys have been demolished. Fred Dibner has had the job of bringing a lot of them down.

During one of the summer holidays we decided to have a lovely country walk with Joyce and her family, and Ruth came too. We decided to start a little distance away and take two cars as there were 7 of us. They arrived in Horwich at my house about 10 o'clock and I was just finishing off the picnic and chores. The three children jumped into the back of our car, thinking that I was driving, and then John casually walked out and got into the driving seat. I couldn't say, "You can't drive", because he had been driving far longer than me since before driving tests were required. So Jim and Joyce said,

"Oh! You had better get in our car."

John had to lead as he knew the way going through Blackrod to Worthington Lakes. As we reached the cross roads the lights were on red and he stopped, with us behind. The lights changed to green but the car in front of John stalled and did not get going until the lights were changing again. Unfortunately, John did not notice and tried to move forwards across the road. He was hit by a car travelling fast from the right. It caught the rear and the car spun round twice, ending up facing backwards. Now Joyce and Jim were sitting in the car behind and witnessed the crash; both their children were inside the car. It was horrendous. They jumped out and ran across; all the traffic stopped.

Hazel and Ruth were crying but James was unconscious. John seemed stunned but unhurt. We got the girls out onto the grass verge and waited for the ambulance. So they all ended up in hospital. We were very lucky; Ruth, Hazel and John were quite bumped and bruised; Hazel still has a lump on her cheek to this day, but James had a fractured mandible and needed an operation. He was in intensive care for a while but was allowed to go home, with his jaw wired up. He couldn't eat for several weeks, only fluids, and lost a lot of weight so Joyce became anxious trying to make him take nourishing drinks. I went and bought him a bottle of cheap lemonade which he downed right away! He was 11 years old and so he had to start at his new school with his mouth wired up.

Eventually they received some compensation from my car insurance. The police came to see John and said that he had to rescind his licence and no more driving. They said that he had had a good innings of driving, and took his licence away. The car was written off, it was in my name so all the expense had to come off my insurance. I even received a bill from the ambulance service but as long as the children recovered, little else mattered.

Surprisingly, about nine months later, I received a phone call and the man who was calling asked me if I was the last owner of this beautiful black VW. He wanted to buy it for his daughter's 21st birthday. He was very concerned to learn whether it had been in an accident and thought it looked too good to be true. I said that it had been in an accident but not that it had been a right-off. He thanked me for being honest but I don't know who bought the car later. It just goes to show – if something looks too good to be true, it probably is!

Marjorie and Philip

The grandchildren are growing past school age, and thinking of moving on – I have eight in various age groups – Marjorie's three girls, Sarah, Ruth and Judith; Joyce's two children, Hazel and James, and then Christine, Heidi and Joseph, Jeannette's three. I have mentioned some of the paths they have taken, and will now continue with Marjorie.

She had been separated from John for about six years. One day every year, the university had an open day to receive all the students for the next year, covering different career opportunities. She was having a break after a very busy morning, when a man was passing. He stopped and had a chat with her, then went on his way. At these events, usually a dinner is arranged for all the staff, so when all the business is complete, they change and go up for dinner, with the tables all set with place names for each.

When Marjorie arrived, she was placed next but one to this chap she had chatted with at the break time. Having met once, they started a friendship and eventually, after some years, got married! They have a house in Chorley, but mostly they live in Spain, having bought a villa there, and their children and families often have holidays out there.

They have now been married for more than 10 years and spend much of their time abroad in America and on holiday as well as in Spain.

When Sarah and Nigel and the two children Benjamin and Jessica were going on holiday to Spain, they asked me if I would like to join them. I often minded the children at home and took them to school in the morning so thought I could be useful on holiday too.

The day for travelling was very wet and windy and during the flight it became very stormy. On nearing the airport at Barcelona the plane began rolling and dipping in the wind and we were told to put seat belts on and attach any young children to their parents. We circled the airport three times and everyone went silent, you could have heard a pin drop! The plane swayed up and down but eventually, after great difficulty, it landed safely and we all began to breathe again. When we got off the plane, we had to keep hold of each other as the wind was so strong; it was blowing the palm trees right over on both sides of us.

However, after a two hour drive, we arrived at this beautiful villa in the mountains above Alcossebre, complete with a swimming pool and all the equipment needed such as rubber dinghy, floats, lifebelts. This villa also has a tennis court and table tennis room and we made full use of everything during our stay. Ben was about 8 years old and Jess 5; they could both swim very well. I could just about swim one length but one time as I was swimming up, Jessica dived in and landed on my back. I felt that I was drowning but Sarah was in the pool and has a life savers certificate, so grabbed hold of me and helped me to the side.

There was a large veranda with a big oval table where we had most of our meals, at the side of the pool. It looked out over the Mediterranean, what a view!

After being out one day we all decided to have a late swim; the pool lights up from underneath. While we were in the water, it started to thunder and lightning, so with lights above and lights below, it was very exciting.

Another day when we were in the pool, Marjorie somehow managed to get tangled up in the ropes for the pool cover at the deep end. She was just starting to panic and we noticed there was something wrong. Jessica was the first to dive in to her rescue. She swam up to Marjorie and held on to her, whilst treaded water hard enough to keep them both afloat, and thus Marjorie managed to get herself untangled. Jess was a real hero that day, and saved her Nan's life!

Alcossebre has a large harbour with lots of private yachts. The children hired bicycles to ride around the harbour; it was lovely. Then we went to a bullfight arena, not to see a bull killed, but to watch the matadors getting near the bulls and taunting them. There was a table in wood, with steps each side and they would run down the steps to tantalize the bulls. When they were chasing the men, the bulls ran up the steps on to the table but the men had places they could hide behind, out of too much danger. We had a very interesting time and I was chatting to the Spanish families on either side. We were reluctant to leave.

More Changes

My husband John celebrated his 90th birthday in style. We invited all our friends and family to visit us at home and had a lovely birthday cake. John was very pleased with being the centre of attention. However, he was starting to become a bit forgetful and frail.

One afternoon we had been sitting in the garden, when I went in the kitchen to put some potatoes in the oven for tea. The lawn has three steps up - it is on a higher level, and as I was sorting out the vegetables, I heard a crash. I ran into the garden to find John on the concrete path. He had walked off the lawn wall and crashed his head on the wall opposite, and was bleeding profusely. I managed to get him up, put a large towel on the bleeding, and rang 999. Within a short while the ambulance arrived and drove all the way to hospital with the siren sounding. I stayed with him until 7pm.

It was diagnosed that he had suffered a stroke, not just the fall. He was in hospital for four weeks before he died. He was buried in the grave with his first wife and her family, there being one place left in the deeds.

So I went back to living on my own again. We had had ten eventful years!

I by now had completed fifteen years with the W.R.V.S., the point at which we receive a medal with a ribbon. It has the same colours as the Defence Corps, as it is remotely connected to that corps. I was now working in the hospital shop at the Royal Bolton Hospital. It had been having extensions and alterations. They now had a new, very modern shop, and I was offered a job on the tills. I worked on there, very much enjoying it.

After living on my own for a number of years I caught, as I thought, the 'flu. I felt quite ill during the night, so decided I would ring the doctor's next morning, to go and get some antibiotics, then I would feel much better. I thought I had better take the car to the doctor's, because the road has quite a steep hill. This was winter and very cold, and the surgery would be busy with patients. I rang the doctor's and they asked who I would like to see, being a group practice. I said anyone who was available - all I wanted was a quick appointment, some antibiotics, and back to bed.

I drove the car down, parked it and went in. When my name was called, I struggled a bit. The doctor started to examine me and said,

"Will you come through to this room, for a special test?"

Before he had finished he said,

"You are going into hospital now."

"I haven't got anything with me!"

"I have rung for the ambulance and it's on its way. Your blood pressure is sky high!"

"None of my family know I am ill!"

"Just give me one phone number."

So I gave him Sarah's number, as she was the only one who lived near. So I was rushed to Bolton Royal, and put on oxygen immediately. I felt as though I was in a dream. I was diagnosed with pneumonia. Then at visiting time that evening half the family arrived saying,

"Why didn't you ring us and say you were ill?"

They were excellent in hospital. I was in one week. As they were so busy and desperate for beds, I was looked after at home by the family. Then Marjorie said,

> "I don't think you should continue to work at the hospital, you are getting older and more vulnerable to infections. Try something different if you still like doing voluntary work."

So I didn't go back to work at the hospital shop. A few months later I had an appointment with the local podiatry clinic, and I was sitting in the waiting area, where it had a big poster saying,

> "Can you spare at least one hour per week for visiting the sick or elderly?"

It had the number of the office to ring.

> "Yes," I said to myself, "I will do that!"

When I called at the office, they explained the need for visiting at this stage of life. With the progress of travel, money and education, the children of today have more opportunities. They have further education in lots of cases, so need to choose which university teaches the subjects required. Then, having left home and completed their goal, have to apply for a career job. It's then where they are accepted that they go to live, so very rarely go back home to live – not like in our early days when all lived in the same neighbourhood. So that is great, when Mum and Dad are still working and living a full life. It's later when one falls ill or dies, when we hear of the lonely elderly people.

Now this visiting service is very good, as the visitees can have days out that we arrange, meals out, and a visitor who calls each week. It makes life more pleasant, as one's own children are not so near, and often working full time and don't have enough time for the oldies. At the moment I have three ladies who I visit each week and take an interest in.

This scheme also offers courses to attend. We think we know it all until we realize the finer points we need to know! I have

E.A.Pierce June 2008

earned a few certificates since joining, but I call them the bottom of the ladder for me.

I actually received a nice letter from the W.R.V.S. with now, a badge inside covering 20 years service. That completes my active service with the W.R.V.S.

A Knitting Nancy

Our church now has a "shoebox full of useful presents" scheme, to go to the needy countries each year. So, many of the congregation knit hats, scarves or jumpers, to go in these shoe boxes. Added are soap, tooth brushes, pencils, note books, and various little toys. This scheme has snowballed and large wagons collect all the shoe boxes, which we wrap in Christmas paper, and pay £2 towards transport. They go to places like Bosnia and Albania. So since this scheme has taken off, we regularly collect or buy wool. So I thought it a good idea to start my visitees knitting. The scarves are straight-forward to knit, so I get them started, and it's another interest for them. Most of them have knitted in their prime anyway.

Here I must divert to reach the point of my story.

Sarah, my granddaughter, when she was at Bolton College doing design engineering, met Nigel, who was on the same course. Now Nigel came from Southern Ireland, County Cork, from a farming family. So as time went on, Sarah and Nigel got married in Ireland. It was a lovely wedding; we all went over.

We were all introduced to Nigel's family, and became friendly. His parents went to the same sort of church as us; in fact his dad, yet another John, was a church warden. Well as the summers passed, Sarah invited them to come to England. I don't think they had been here before, and as I had a spare room in my house, they stayed with me at night and went over to Nigel and Sarah's during the day. As time passed, Nigel's parents were reaching retirement, so his brothers Gordon and Victor began to run the farm. John, Nigel's dad, still came over to visit us on his own each year, and here's where we go back to the knitting. He still stayed at my house, as I had the spare room, and went over to Nigel's each day.

Now my next door neighbour, Rhoda was getting older, and living on her own, so I quite often went in to see her, and of course, started her knitting. John, when he came over from Ireland, would go into Rhoda's and chat. (He was very broad Irish, and we did have some trouble understanding him when he was talking fast!) Well would you believe it! We went in one night, and she was knitting, and she had got into a fix with it, and lost some stitches. John said,

"Give it to me, I'll fix it."

I said,

"Can you knit?"

— a big farmer! He took it and sorted it out for her.

Then I said,

"Right! If you can knit, and now have time, could you do some scarves for the Christmas shoe boxes?"

He agreed, and we came back, and I found him some needles and wool, and he was delighted!

When he returned back home, Nigel's sister Deidre, rang Sarah and asked,

"What have you done to my dad? He is sitting knitting all the time like a sissy!"

John now knits the length in different colours, and I finish them off by putting a multi-coloured fringe on each end. I may add, he knitted 64 scarves last year, and they all went to Romania – and we could have done with more! This year, as Nigel went over to visit, he brought back another 30 for me to finish so far, and so it goes on. Wonderful! Being retired, and all the boys running the farm he seems to like doing it, and it helps poor orphan children.

Talking about orphan children, we also have an ongoing service for little children in Albania, who are in hospitals. A couple of men visited this children's hospital a few years ago, and were saddened to see the little ones, some orphaned, lying in these beds without even a toy, so they went and bought a few teddies, and these children hugged them – the first thing they had ever owned. So a friend, Kath, and I knit these teddies. She does the main body in colours, and I sew them up and embroider the faces, and we believe each child now receives a teddy on entering hospital, and it has been noted they improve more quickly, having something to cuddle.

There are always some voluntary things people could do for others.

Rule of Thumb

I also deliver a number of magazines from the church each month. Then last year, I had just reached the last house with the magazines when I tripped up; my toe caught in the projecting edge of this concrete step, and down I went! There was a rather large tree at the side, so no-one saw me. I picked myself up and thought to myself,

"That wasn't too bad!"

But when I looked at my hand, my thumb bone was protruding right out at an angle. I was taken aback. I went home, got a clean bandage, wrapped it over my thumb and round my hand, collected a *'Reader's Digest'*, my glasses and purse, all to go in my bag, and proceeded to go on two buses to the hospital.

When I arrived, it was seething with people, so I sat down and waited to be seen. Two hours of reading later, my name was called, so I went into this cubicle. The doctor took one look and sent me to the x-ray department. Over there, I sat for another hour, with folks going in and out. Finally done, I went back to A&E, and sat for another age, until I was called in to the cubicle again.

The doctor tried to put my thumb back, but it was too painful, so he gave me some gas and air, and tried again. It was no use, so he gave me an injection and tried again. Still hopeless! He rang for the consultant to give his advice. He came and took a look.

"Stop doing any more. She will have to be admitted and have it done in theatre."

"Oh no!"

I thought. I had hoped to be back home at tea time, and no-one would even know. But I then had to wait to be admitted. We had reached 7pm, and I had to wait until after visiting time had passed. I didn't have any phone numbers with me, and couldn't quite remember Sarah's. I did know it, but at times like that... I just couldn't think!

So I was duly settled in to a ward, and they gave me a drink, but nothing to eat because of the anaesthetic. I had a chat to another patient, then read for a while. Then the doctor in green came to me, and explained what he was going to do. I eventually went into theatre at 2am in the morning. I don't remember any more, until I woke up the next day at about 7 or 8 o'clock. The nurse said I could have some breakfast. My hand was all bandaged up with a big hook popping out. Then the phone rang about 9 o'clock and the nurse said,

> "Your granddaughter is on the phone and you are in trouble!"

What had happened, Sarah had rung my house in connection with her children, as I would mind them before school occasionally. As she had got no answer, and it being early in the morning, she went to my house. She had a key and let herself in.
No Nan? She went upstairs. Bed not slept in? She rang her mother and sister, and finally the police. They asked if she had rung friends and family, then suggested she now try the hospitals. She was mortified to find me in the Royal Hospital!

When I answered the phone, it was Ruth, Sarah's sister. She started getting annoyed with me, for not letting them know, and then said she would come and collect me. (Before they found out, I had been planning to get a taxi home, and keep it quiet!) However I did tell Ruth not to go on at me, as I was a patient, and only just coming to! So Ruth brought me home.

I must tell you here, that I had thought of changing my car. I didn't want a brand new one, so I was happy when Jeannette came and said they were selling their second car. It was only a few years old, and in good order. It so happened that this was the day we'd arranged that she and Karl would drive both cars over to me, leave the car I was buying with me, and go back home in the other.

So I had to get in my new car, and drive it around the area with Jeannette, to give me all the instructions one needs, that very same day as Ruth bringing me back from the hospital. So shortly after I arrived home, Jeannette and Karl arrived, and I had very little choice, with my hand all bandaged up! I could just manage to turn the ignition key. We had a run round, and it was raining of course! Later in the week I had it overhauled and sorted out the price, after selling my old car. It's a Peugeot, and fingers crossed, it's doing fine!

I had been having some gear box trouble with the previous car, which I had bought second hand. It was half suggested that it could be my fault now, as I was getting older and losing height (not that it could have been a fault in the car before I bought it!) I began to get a bit bothered, so Nigel, Sarah's husband, said to me,

"Would you like me to give you a test drive?"

I agreed. I had been driving for 40 years, and thought if I did have some problems, I would call it a day and give up driving. So Nigel came round one day, about 5pm, a busy time. I got into the car quite apprehensive, wondering. We went all round Horwich for about three quarters of an hour, and back home. With great trepidation I got out, waiting for the verdict. Then to my surprise, he said,

"There is nothing wrong with your driving at all!"

So that gave me the confidence to carry on.

E.A.Pierce June 2008

The tables are turned

I have mentioned about the holidays we spent in Blaenau Ffestiniog in the mountainous area of Snowden in North Wales when Marjorie and John had a Welsh cottage. Their children were all school age then and we played among the sand hills of Harlech and around the coast. We spent time at Porthmadoc and went to the little station where we could get a steam train up through the mountains to Ffestiniog.

Now, of course, my grandchildren, all eight of them, have finished their education and have moved on with their careers and living independent lives. I never fail to be amazed at how fast time moves on and these young children, whom I took out and about, have invited me to go and stay with them. How the tables have turned!

Heidi, who lives in Berkhamsted and is now a director of music, invited me to stay at her home for a week at the same time as her brother, Joe, was visiting. They all have their own cars so I went down on the train and was looked after and taken out every day.

We visited Windsor Castle, various places in and around Oxford and went into London to see Buckingham Palace and a show at the theatre. London being so very busy, we travelled on the underground, it was so fast. One puts a card in a machine, the barrier lifts and one makes a dash for the platform to jump on a train, which is always very full. We had to watch for the station, to jump out; and when crossing the road, Heidi and Joe would grab my hands and run me across.

I felt as though I was living in a backwater when got home to Horwich, it was so peaceful, but I did enjoy the holiday.

Later that year Joseph, who is living in Guernsey and working in the bank, invited me and his other grandma (who, you may recall, is also called Edith) to have a week with him. What a beautiful island! When I rang him to ask if we would be near the sea side, he said that it's just near the bottom of every road! We flew down to Guernsey. He would call for us in his car and take us on scenic trips; we covered the whole island that week. We did lots of lovely walks and dined out most days, although Joe cooked some great meals for us too.

Then Ruth, who lived for 8 years in Edinburgh, in Scotland, also asked me to stay with her for a holiday. She lived in Queensferry, by the Forth Bridge and worked for Scottish Telecom. We had a wonderful holiday, visited the Castle and walked along the Royal Mile and learned quite a lot of history. She is back home in Bolton now and married with a family.

James, is now a doctor in the North East, specialising in Orthopaedics. I visited him a few times, usually with his mum and dad, but Joyce and I had a holiday with him at his house near Hexham and covered quite a bit of Hadrian's Wall. His house bordered onto farmland and we did some lovely rural walks and dined out. It is so nice to see where they live.
Joyce and I had another few days with Heidi this year in Berkhamsted and while we were there had the opportunity to see Hazel. She has moved to Walton on Thames in Surrey, with her partner Martin. They made us a lovely roast dinner, beautifully set out with all the trimmings and showed us their beautiful large garden before we left for home. It was quite a journey going back up North from there.

Sarah hasn't moved further afield but has moved house a number of times. She it was who served her time with engineering, but after she was married and had children, it proved difficult to continue. When the children went to school, she worked as a doctor's receptionist but now is training in a solicitor's office.

We thought Judith would train as a chef as she was so keenly interested in cooking fancy meals. When her mother Marjorie entertained, Judith would prepare all the courses, and the meal was always a great success. However, she has an interesting job with Salford Social Services and lives in Bolton with her partner, Paul.

Now Christine, who trained as a nursery nurse, is living near Crewe. She is married to Eddie and they have three children. She is hoping to move soon to Rhyl, in Wales where Eddie is starting a new job as a church pastor. I expect at some time that I will go and visit them there, so travelling isn't finished yet!

Bringing you up to date

My second daughter, Joyce, was teaching maths at a college when she decided to do her Masters degree with Open University. Then she became Head of the Mathematics department. She also took on training the students for the Duke of Edinburgh Award Scheme, and was very successful. She took early retirement in 2007 and is now a Magistrate.

Then Jeannette, after some years with the shop in Blackburn, went back into teaching, and Karl then thought he would like to do a course in Theology, so applied to the Elim Bible College in Nantwich, near Crewe. They all moved house and went to live in Nantwich, and the children all changed schools, and progressed from there.

One sunny afternoon, they went for a walk on the public footpath across the grounds of Willaston Hall, just local. It was quiet, with no-one else around. Some horses were kept in the grounds, and one of them came across to them very purposefully. They tried to ignore it, and walked on, but it suddenly came up behind them and pushed Jeannette over, then stood over her trying to bite her face. She tried pushing it away, but it was unrelenting. She bashed it on the nose, at which point it put one foot on her chest, and she couldn't move. Karl tried his best to push it away, but had never handled horses, and was now frightened to upset it further and cause more damage to Jeannette.

She told him he must run to the road and flag down help. (This was before the days of mobile phones.) Short of options, he did this, and thankfully a car quickly stopped, whose owner could handle horses, and he was able to rescue her. She had a fair few bruises that night, but mercifully no serious injuries.

They contacted the police, as school children often walked across that footpath coming home from school, and the horse was put down. The owner was not in the mind to give compensation however – not even a new coat (which was ruined!)

Jeannette has now been teaching Special Needs children for many years. And now, most of the grandchildren are in different parts of the country, following their own careers.

Last summer I booked a holiday to Llandudno with Doris. I drove the car. We had a lovely time, and went up the passes by Snowdonia, then drove home. I was disgusted that I picked up a speeding ticket in Wales! The camera filmed me doing 35 m.p.h. in a 30 m.p.h. zone. I have to say that it was in the middle of the countryside and anyone would have expected it to be a 40 zone, at least. I hope I didn't break any records – like the oldest driver with a speeding fine!

I don't do any long journeys now. I go to visit Joyce and Jim every Friday at Ashton-under-Lyne, which is about thirty miles, and I enjoy that. I stay the night, because their children have moved on, so they have a spare room, and as I am now older they think it is better, particularly when the dark nights in winter arrive. It would be difficult if I had any problems with the car in the dark on my own.

I am beginning now to feel quite old, now that my grandchildren are producing their own offspring. Sarah has Benjamin and Jessica, aged 11 years and 8 years old, and after all that time has just had another little girl name Gabriella – they are all lovely children. When Ruth married Pete, he already had three girls to his first wife – another Jessica, then Madeleine and Emily. She had her first son Jenson, who is now 5, and just recently a second boy, Jameson. Next is Jeannette's eldest daughter, Christine. She married Eddie and they have Aidan who is 6, Callum who is 3, and Isla who is 1 year old. So that gives me eleven great-grandchildren!

Epilogue

One wall in my living room is almost completely covered in pictures of my family celebrating their academic achievements. I have been to so many graduations that I have lost count. Opposite them I have all the wedding and baby photos. I find it amazing that all this stems from Harold and me!

I cannot believe how the world has altered in my lifetime. There have been advances in science and engineering that have changed how we travel, build and communicate, especially using computers. Research in medicine has increased our age expectancy and improved treatment for many illnesses which were previously incurable. We take for granted the use of antibiotics which would have saved many people from the pneumonia epidemic in the year I was born.

The trees at the Memorial Pinetum near Rivington Pike were all planted in memory of beloved family members. There is a record book kept in the 'Little Barn' at Rivington where all the

My two special trees at the Pinetum, Rivington

names and dates are listed, so that the trees can be identified.

You will probably have guessed who my two trees are for!

One is for my husband, Harold, as there is no grave stone to mark his passing.

The other one is for John. Although it was for his 90th birthday as he was still alive then, it seemed very appropriate as he so loved being out and about in the countryside always, and he was delighted with the idea of a special tree. When we walked along that way, I used to avoid the area so that he would not see that all the other trees were for memorials, in case he thought I had been a bit premature!

It will be my 90th birthday soon, so I have covered almost a century from the days I started on skates, progressed onto a bike, then car and now aeroplane travel. So many changes and so many stories to tell! My children, having listened to many of the tales said,

>"Why don't you write a book?"

And so this is it.

When looking back to before the Industrial Revolution, what vast steps have taken place! I wonder what man's brain will produce in the future! Whether for better or worse, we don't know. I do remember my mother often saying,

>"I don't like what is happening these days. I am glad I am going this way out."

And sometimes I find myself wondering the same.

E.A.Pierce June 2008

This book is dedicated to my very dear daughters, to pass on to their children.

My family has been shown where the trees are; my prayer is that they will find hope and inspiration from them, and from my stories, whatever the future holds.

With all my love, Mum.